This book could not have been written without the financial assistance of the Scottish Arts Council and the expertise and advice of Don Hurley

Acclaim for A. L. Kennedy's
On Bullfighting

"As artful as a matador's final pass." —*Esquire*

"Mesmerizingly well written . . . A subtle, wonderfully controlled yet deeply affecting essay on life as a ceaseless struggle against the dominion of death . . . A thrilling and thought-provoking read."
—John Banville, The Irish Times

"Brilliantly tense." —*The Observer*

"Informative, minutely observed and beautifully written."
—The Independent

"Typically incisive, it . . . shows why [A. L. Kennedy] remains one of the most compelling writers of her generation." —*The Scotsman*

ALSO BY A. L. KENNEDY

Night Geometry and the Garscadden Trains
Looking for the Possible Dance
Now That You're Back
Original Bliss
So I Am Glad

A. L. Kennedy

On Bullfighting

A. L. Kennedy, the author of three novels and two short story collections, has received six awards for her writing, including the Somerset Maugham Award, the John Llewellyn Rhys Prize, and the Encore Award. She lives in Glasgow.

On Bullfighting

A. L. Kennedy

ANCHOR BOOKS
A Division of Random House, Inc.
New York

FIRST ANCHOR BOOKS EDITION, APRIL 2001

Copyright © 1999 by A. L. Kennedy

All rights reserved under International and Pan-American Copyright
Conventions. Published in the United States by Anchor Books, a
division of Random House, Inc., New York. Originally published
in hardcover in Great Britain by Yellow Jersey, a division of
Random House UK, London, in 1999.

Anchor Books and colophon are trademarks of Random House, Inc.

Library of Congress Cataloging-in-Publication Data

Kennedy, A. L.
On bullfighting / A. L. Kennedy.
p.   cm.
Includes bibliographical references.
ISBN 0-385-72081-5 (pbk.)
1. Bullfights.   I. Title.
GV1107.K45 2001
791.8'2—dc21   00-060587

www.anchorbooks.com

Printed in the United States of America
10   9   8   7   6   5   4   3   2

Contents

Contents

On Bullfighting

Chapter One

An Introduction to Death

I'm thinking I might actually enjoy this, if I had more time.

It's Sunday, the first day of the week: the one that's for resting and possibly talking to God, but I am doing neither. I am sitting across my window ledge and thinking that Sundays are always much the same: vaguely peaceful and emptied and smug: and I am looking out over my gutter and four storeys down to my street. It's late in a mild afternoon and there are flickers of spring in the trees. The smell of young grass drifts up to me from the park and the air is also coloured very slightly with waking earth and sunny masonry. Cars beetle past, roofs gleaming, but there's no one out walking. Although I'd expect there might be on such a pleasant day, there is no one about.

Which means I should do this. I should jump now, while I can.

Because I don't want anyone looking, or there to be hurt by me when I fall. It's only me I want to kill. And I don't wish to be gawped at while I'm killing. I believe I've had enough embarrassment for one life.

But I can do this now, it's all clear, no observers—I can jump.

Not that I feel despairing—I don't—not any more. I'm not even remotely upset: I am only very heavy, only that. I have turned into something new, unworkably substantial, too solid to last. I'm already straining my grip on the window frame, finding it hard to keep myself above the street.

So I should go.

I wanted to do this naked. There aren't many things I like to do undressed, but I did want to leave life as I met it, because that seemed neat and I can be neat if I choose to, on this day of all days. And because, with no clothes to disguise me, there would be no more pretence that I'm anything more than function, mechanics, butcher's shop window stuff. I would like to think otherwise, but currently, I don't.

Still, the thought of myself on the pavement with my skin against the stone—the idea of that little discomfort, which I wouldn't even feel—made me squeamish. It made climbing up to the window too difficult. So I've kept on my clothes and made the climb. But I have taken off my shoes.

The only proper eccentricity I've managed to cultivate in all this time: I take off my shoes to do anything important, it helps me concentrate. I always, for example, used to get shoeless before I wrote. And this is pretty unimpressive, I do know, as a trick of personality, I had hoped for something more: like keeping a parrot that screamed obscenities, or randomly screaming obscenities myself, or perhaps just affecting an eye-catching limp. When I was a kid I would secretly practise all kinds of limp.

But it's rather too late for that kind of nonsense now.

I look at the sky and it's all a broad, dumb blue. I bought this flat because I could finally afford one and it felt happy and had a study where I could write—my first ever study—and because it had high windows that showed nothing but the sky.

I should really go.

And now I have been in this flat and unhappy for far longer than I'd have wished. Which is of no particular consequence to anyone much beyond myself. I do know that. The inadequacy of my misery hasn't escaped me, the fact that I'm literally boring myself to death. This all started with such utterly commonplace stuff, things other people can manage and that I should have managed, too: a man that I loved has died and another has hurt me, I am not in good health and don't sleep, I have a rather averagely broken heart and no more need for the flat someone else would be glad of, or for its study, because I don't write. I'm a writer who doesn't write and that makes me no one at all. I don't look very different, but I have nothing of value inside.

So why stay here, when I have no further use.

Although this proves that I am a coward, I close my eyes before making what I hope will be my last voluntary move.

And then the music starts.

By this I don't mean that the music of my past life is dashing down to flutter by my ears, or that I experience some kind of filmic interlude, or the hymns of choirs angelic, demonic, or revelatory. I mean that I hear a man's voice droning from a distance, cheaply amplified and criminally flat and singing what has always been my least favourite folk song in all of the world—*Mhairi's Wedding*.

For those of you lucky enough to have never encountered this piece of pseudo-Celtic pap I will say that it's first words are *Step we gaily, on we go, heel for heel and toe for toe*, and that it then deteriorates. It mentions—I can hear it fucking mentioning—herring and oatmeal and peat and several other rustic elements vital to the noble, rural, ceilidhing Gaelic life.

I had to sing *Mhairi's Wedding* in school music lessons for, if recollection serves me, thirty or forty years. I need hardly say that its tune, what there is of it, is precisely annoying enough to be utterly unforgettable without having a single moment of genuine muscle, emotion or charm. I have never truly liked anybody called Mhairi, quite simply because of this song.

But here it is, coming from nowhere that I can see, from nowhere that makes any sense, from some unlikely outdoor concert, some especially elaborate practical joke. Verse and chorus, it spindrifts in towards me from the suburbs and the carriageway to the west and it breaks the day. I can't do this any more. I can't wait here and listen to *Mhairi's Wedding* and still prepare myself to die with even a rag of credibility. Equally, I can't face jumping while the bloody thing is still being sung. Murdering myself to this accompaniment is more than I can bear. So now I can't even die. It seems that, having been fucked over by every other part of my existence, I am now being splendidly, finally fucked by either divine intervention or simple chance.

I get back down into my living room and I put on my shoes and I stand for a while, having nowhere else to go, and I cry, because the life I had hoped I would not have to meet with again is still here and still waiting and still mine. Divine intervention wasn't something I happened to want.

Oh, and do feel free to imagine my unparalleled delight whenever I remember that *Mhairi's Wedding* is, at least in part, why I'm alive and typing this today.

And, just in case you've wondered, I only mention these things by way of a preamble because this book will be, at least in part, about people who risk death for a living. Whatever you or I think of how and why they do this, they are making that commitment every working day—a commitment which I'm pointing out I know that I can't equal. But my little confession of a contemplated sin is intended to indicate that I will give you as much as I can. I do promise that.

I will tell you about bulls, the *toros bravos* of Spain, bred to be killed in the ring as the culmination of the three acts which form the *corrida de toros*.* There are, in the world, many other bull spectacles—U.S. rodeo confrontations, Portuguese and French displays of arena athleticism, Spanish *charlotadas*, or "comic" plaza circuses, and *rejoneos* where mounted *rejoneadors* use lances to kill bulls, there are bulls set to fight or race other bulls in the Far East—but the traditional, Spanish corrida will

---

*Literally, a running of the bulls, harking back to more disorganised, rural fiestas with elements in common with the current annual running of the bulls towards a ring in Pamplona. It is now the name attached to a traditional Spanish "bullfight."

be the subject of this book. I will focus on the meetings
between bulls and matadors, unmounted men.

And I will point out now that the corrida is not, accu-
rately speaking, a bullfight, although this is the standard
English term for it. No man, as has often been noted,
can actually *fight* half a ton or so of bull. What happens
in the ring is more complicated, repellent, fascinating,
grotesque, sacramental, ugly, ritualistic, haphazard,
sacred and blasphemous than any fight.

I will use a glossary and footnotes,* which attempt to
translate or at least to explain the vocabulary of the corrida; the particular, peculiar, partly gypsy, fastidiously
detailed and occasionally mystical language in which the
corrida has come to be defined. And I will write about
the *toreros*,[†] the men (and the handful of women) whose
job it is to kill the bulls and who may, themselves, be
killed by bulls. Such deaths are infrequent, particularly
in these days of effective antibiotics, but they are still by
no means impossible. Toreros must also accustom themselves to a career which will inevitably involve injury by
goring: sometimes serious, if not grotesque, goring. No
matter what your personal opinion of the corrida may
happen to be, these facts are inescapable: in the corrida,
bulls and men meet fear and pain and both may die.

The proximity of so much dying tends to demand a
certain honesty from observers. So, in the spirit of my
earlier promise, I will be honest with you. As a former

---

*Something I hate. Sadly, some subjects demand them. Sorry.
[†]*Torero*, sometimes used interchangeably with *matador*, properly applies
to any of the three classes of human participants in the corrida—the
matador who kills the bull, the *picador* who is mounted and tests the bull
with spear-thrusts, and the *peones* who assist the matador and must draw
bulls away from fallen or terror-struck men.

author and former suicide, honesty's about all I have left. Which means that I can tell you this book does not come from any prior interest or enthusiasm on my part. I have no love for the hairy, manly Hemingway approach to the corrida, no anxious need to lurk at the bedsides of wounded toreros, fiddling with the dressings on tight, young thighs. I am not a woman who finds the facts of death erotic (although we will discuss such matters in due course) and the sight of boys in spangled satin and slippers stiff-legging it through their required paces does nothing for me, per se.

I was simply asked if I would write this and I simply agreed. When I began the necessary research, I could have heard that the corrida had been banned throughout the world for ever and ever amen and I would have remained unconcerned. I came to this with entirely selfish motives. I wanted to see if I was still capable of writing anything at all. I wanted to keep my mind occupied, because—left to its own devices—it might very well manage to kill, or at least torment me. And I wanted to discover if the elements which seemed so much a part of the corrida—death, transcendence, immortality, joy, pain, isolation and fear—would come back to me. Because they were part of the process of writing and, good and bad, I miss them.

I will try to make this book as accurate as I can, although there are others that any would-be *aficionado** might do better to consult: they're listed in the bibliography. For those who are already implacably repulsed by

*Literally, someone who has a liking for anything, or who is a fan of anything. Quite often used specifically of those who have a knowledge of and enthusiasm for the corrida.

the corrida, I don't wish to change your mind, but I may be informative and it's certainly always my policy to know my enemy—it may also be yours. For those of you who are already gripped by *afición;** I can't even promise to inform, in fact, I will probably irritate. You may well be enraged by my attempt to anatomise your passion and, like experts the world over, may well be keen to enjoy correcting an interloper's mistakes. Whoever you are, you and I both know that you're the reader—this book is, therefore, yours to do with as you'd like. It is a record of both the progress and the conclusions of a relatively brief study of the corrida. It is a personal view. If you feel this will not suit you, you can, of course, leave now.

But before we begin in earnest with the bulls I will add a postscript to my window-sill interlude.

A few months after I studied the pavement and then didn't meet it, I was talking to a friend of mine who is an undertaker and also a writer: or a writer and also an undertaker, depending on your frame of mind. When I told him how much I still wanted to die, to finish up the job, he said—and I do remember this exactly, "Don't do that, Alison. You would look so silly." He had guessed, quite correctly, that the last thing I'd want my death to be is silly.

This is, naturally, why the strains of *Mhairi's Wedding* stopped me jumping—dying in time to that tune would

---

*The quality of liking, having one's fancy taken by something. Again it can be used specifically to denote an informed, even opinionated, passionate interest in the corrida. To have it is to be an initiate in taurine circles, to be a believer.

have been entirely ridiculous and I wanted to keep my dignity. Or, to be more precise, I still had my pride. Undoubtedly, I could see no point in going on—still can't. And I was thoroughly sick of several types of pain—still am—but there was one last hook of interest in life for my ego and me: I very much wanted to make one last, grand gesture and to make it *properly*. If there was nothing else for me to say and no one to listen, in any case, then at least I could find a way to make my death speak.

Then my kind friend made it beautifully plain that I could make myself dead very easily, but not dead and in control, not dead and also eloquent.

Although recent research seems to show that a torero's body chemistry predisposes him, or occasionally her, to crave risk, the average *matador** is not exactly suicidal. He goes into the ring to face both destruction and survival. The matador is at the heart of a strange balance between the demands of safety and of fame, between the instinct for self-preservation and the appetite for the ultimate (and therefore ultimately dangerous) execution of the corrida's three traditional acts. He is both threatened and exalted by a process intended to make death eloquent. The torero, the *cuadrilla*† (the men who sup-

---

*A killer of bulls, as opposed to a butcher, or a murderer of bulls. (Obviously some would think this distinction overly fine.) The matador is the only one permitted to make full passes with the capote de brega and then the muleta and to wear gold decoration on both the jacket and the trousers of his suit. Becoming a torero can be called "taking the gold." All toreros, apart from the picador, wear the *coleta*—a pigtail—as did Roman gladiators.
†The team which supports the matador in the ring. This comprises two *picadors*, three *banderilleros* (also known as *peones*) and the *mozo de espada*, or sword boy, and his assistant.

port him in the ring), the *ganadero* (the rancher who breeds the bulls) and the whole regiment of other interested parties are intended to be held by rules which attempt to make the bull's death more than slaughter, something beyond ten or fifteen minutes of torment and clumsy flight.

Human injury or death also has its place within the fabric of the corrida, and its effects can be ambivalent. While a wound received in the ring may assure one matador's reputation and drive forward his skills, it may destroy the courage of another. The death that stalks all toreros can give their life meaning, offer moments of delirious intensity, even while it drives them into drug abuse, compulsive sexuality and suicide.

And if it does so happen that a human being finds death in the corrida's rarefied afternoon, if a torero, or perhaps one of his cuadrilla, is fatally wounded, then the corrida is intended to redefine the moment of death, to act as our translator. Even the almost always inevitable death of the bull is meant to be controlled within the corrida's physical language, the structure and the sad necessities of its world. The corrida can be seen as an extraordinary effort to elevate the familiar, mysterious slapstick, the irrevocable, indecipherable logic of damage and death, into something almost accessible. The corrida can be seen as both a ritualised escape from destruction and a bloody search for meaning in the end of a life, both an exorcism and an act of faith.

I am not unaware that faith makes living supportable, can make sense out of death, can make any communication both possible and worthwhile. In writing this book,

I am looking for faith. I am not unaware that I need it. I begin with a slender point of connection: that, in attempting to control death, the toreros and I may have a little in common. We have attempted the impossible, something which stands in the face of nature.

And, like many people who feel themselves opposed by forces greater than themselves, I am inclined to be superstitious. Matadors are superstitious, too. Most people have some familiarity with higher and lower types of faith and, when religion seems inadequate or impossibly exalted, we can all resort to courting luck. Every bull ring of any size at all offers some variety of space set aside for toreros who wish to pray and, beyond prayer, toreros and the members of their cuadrillas have patterns and layers of habits and charms to coax in and secure good luck.

Contrary to theatrical tradition, it is not considered unlucky to wish a matador good luck—which is to say, "*Suerte.*"* Not uncoincidentally, the same word describes each of the three stages of the corrida. Even the most talented matador, the most talented "killer of bulls," would acknowledge that each gesture with the bull, successfully completed, is a concrete proof of not only skill, but also good fortune. A matador of any standing draws his confidence from both and then puts

---

*Variously defined as (good) luck, fortune, chance, destiny, lot. *Una suerte de capa* is a cape pass. *Cargar la suerte*—a highly charged phrase, almost impossible to define, even literally. Means something like "to carry/load/bear a pass." Very loosely it would mean the flowing performance of passes in absolute good faith, according to whichever style the observer thinks best. It has also been elegantly translated as "pushing your luck."

himself at risk, while in a condition of acute readiness. Throughout the corrida, he must be as alert and prepared as his training and disposition can make him, because he cannot know the absolute fact of the bull until he meets it, cannot guarantee his safety until he has struck the killing blow. Even then, he should be wary.

On 30th August 1985 José Cubero Sánchez "El Yiyo" turned his back on a bull he had mortally wounded and, while he acknowledged the crowd's applause, was knocked to the ground by the dying animal. All attempts to distract the bull were unsuccessful and, as its strength failed, it gored its killer where he lay. The bull's right horn entered the matador's heart and its last efforts to toss up his body succeeded only in lifting the man to his feet. For an instant, the dead man and the dead bull both stood on the sand. Then "El Yiyo" walked a few paces and fell. A friend of mine who saw this happen has, quite understandably, never forgotten it.

In his death, "El Yiyo" confirmed an old corrida tradition—that a man who kills a bull which has already killed a man will himself be killed by a bull. "El Yiyo" had stepped in to finish the bull which killed "Paquirri" exactly a year previously in Pozoblanco. The corrida provides a setting intended to display its own blend of chaos and coincidence, chance and death.

But, of course, the torero seeks order, a way to live through the afternoon, or leave it with the required dignity. His aim is to control a bull of which he has no real prior knowledge, to dominate it with style and to conjure up its death correctly. If needs be, he must also present his own injury as perfectly as he can. In this respect, matadors are like the rest of us, naked in the grip of reality—they have to rely on what chance gives them. In the execution of their accepted duties, they make this exposure plain.

And chance will make itself plain, from time to time, without any human assistance. For example, I am filling this page on a Sunday, in the cottage I've borrowed from my friend who writes and undertakes, or undertakes and writes, because it may be a place where I can get well. It is a cottage containing both oatmeal and peat and is not far from a spot on the coast where those so inclined can fish for herring. *Mhairi's Wedding* has crept up and caught me at last, but this reality is far more pleasant than the song's unmelodious fiction.

In the byre next to the cottage there are cows in calf and I will mention now that it so happens cows carry their offspring for nine months, in the way that human beings do. And this morning, while I did what passes for my work, a cow in the byre went under the knife. It turned out that her calf was deformed and dead in the womb: she couldn't give birth and would die without a Caesarean section being performed to remove the corpse.

So the thin song of starlings came out with the sun and I sat here and tried to put one word after another and, now and then, provided hot water for the vet who stood and waited in my doorway. He was wearing a surgical gown and gloves, just as he would if he were operating on a person. His arms were up to the shoulder in blood which might as well have been the blood of a person for all that I could tell. I rinsed the bucket for him and filled it when required and then washed away the blood from round the sink—blood which thickened and darkened and dried in just the way that human blood would—most blood being much the same in these respects.

When the procedure was over, I walked into the byre with the farmer to see the dead calf where it lay, milk-white, something of the spider about it: long legs curled impossibly from its perfect hooves to its oddly small body. It was born without a rib cage, and an uncontained sprawl of purple, glossy organs was spread behind it, forced out through its skin by the pressure of the womb. The calf looked very far from human and barely animal, only incapable of holding life.

Back beside the wall was the cow, entirely alive and standing and chewing impassively, as no human mother could at such a time. Her belly hair was clotted with mud and her own blood, a shaved and sewn scar glinted in her side, made strange by a silvery preparation, painted on to prevent infection.

Both the vet and the farmer had wondered if I should look at these things, in case I was squeamish and because the calf seemed so disturbing, a thing against nature. But of course I looked, because my training and disposition made me look. They always do. So today I saw death and survival among animals and men in a way that might almost have been intended, because my life can be quite eloquent without any special manoeuvring from me: I need only be in it.

Life's definite *sense*, of course, remains nothing if not opaque. For example, the farmer and I sat together after the Caesarean and drank tea and agreed that we didn't know why such things happened: why a cow should survive after being cut wide open, why matter should grow strange inside the womb. The farmer wondered, half-serious, if he hadn't had to lose the calf because he'd been working on too many Sundays—not giving the day an adequate respect. I nodded, half-serious myself, saw him out and then went back to work.

Chapter Two

To Send a Bull from Heaven

I'm in Euroland: stuck in the duty-free limbo of watches as broad as dinner plates and dark glasses shining like insects' eyes from windows stacked with cheap booze, jewellery, cameras, improbably ugly shoes. I'm on my way to find out about bulls, pausing in Brussels Airport and en route to Madrid, sitting and taking notes in a fog of inter-mixing European languages. My situation is not unfamiliar—writers are expected to travel these days: if they don't they can't earn their keep—and one airport is so like another that together they all seem to form a fragmented nation, spattered around the globe in unpleasant instalments.

The only thing that's different about this trip is the pain. I am in extraordinary pain. Punch-drunk with anti-inflammatories, muscle relaxants and I can't quite remember what else, I am still in pain. And there is something almost frightening about this particular hurt, about the recurrent stabbing ache in my shoulders, the presses and twists, the tearing sensation I feel in my arms and the more general horror of picking up my bag which weighs, I've made sure, almost nothing. For the first time in even my overly nervous life I am brooding on the likely loopholes in my travel insurance policy, my imagination thumbing through medically nasty scenarios: being ill in a foreign language, trapped in an abusive hospital with no earnings and soaring bills.

I've passed three months without a proper diagnosis and have one further month to go, but I will eventually discover that I have a displaced disk, high in my spine. The pain is amazing, but won't kill me and is, coincidentally, sited in almost exactly the area which, if I were a *toro bravo*, would be called the *morrillo*—the highly developed head-tossing muscle in the bull's neck. Behind this massive muscle, the mounted *picador* is intended to drive home his lance: the *vara*, and around it the *banderilleros* attempt to place their long, barbed darts: the paper-ruffed *banderillas*. The particularly deep, round ache, which bites in whenever I move my arms, roughly mirrors the bull's *rubios*—which is the name the corrida has given to the ideal point for the matador to place his final, killing sword blow. It's a spot roughly the size of a ten-pence piece where the torero's blade can best enter to find the gap between the bull's substantial shoulder blades, slip through and then slice on down, hopefully avoiding the backbone, to sever the *vena cava*, or one of the pulmonary blood vessels. Contrary to popular belief, bulls that die in the corrida are rarely killed with a stab wound to the heart.

As a credible coincidence in fiction, of course, this wouldn't work. The idea of my leaving for Madrid and

the Las Ventas* plaza while inadvertently acting as
a (barely) walking personification of the corrida's first
two acts would never see the light of day in any self-
respecting novel. I'm recording my airport travails here
because they were a fact—an intervention of chance in
reality—and another proof that God, as an author, has
absolutely no shame and an extremely sophisticated
sense of humour. He notes the fall of sparrows and, in
my opinion, he's also more than fond of irony.

And, as often happens, if I'd fully understood my situation I might have been able to find it amusing. But
instead, I growled off for my second inevitably bumpy
flight of the day on an aeroplane which smelt of vomit
and hot tights. I then welcomed the night in a clean but
threadbare Madrid hotel.

Once there, I lay on my bed while my pain drummed
and crouched behind me and the sounds of the global
village leached in: voices with their words peeled away, a
whine of Brits, a tall-in-the-saddle American duet bluff-
ing by with uneasy laughs and the softer press of Spanish, clipped off by the closing of a door. My tiny, snowy
television showed adverts for Ikea and Burger King:
bland supranational brands from the global market,
sandwiching round a dubbed, Hollywood movie dealing
with events which took place in the Second World
War—a conflict from which Franco's fascist Spain held
itself carefully apart.

---

*The main bull ring in Madrid, more formally known as the Plaza de
Toros Monumental. An arena known for its discerning public, where any
matador must appear to confirm his *alternativa*, or ascension to the level
of full professional.

I wavered towards something like a sleep, thinking that I could appreciate why some Spaniards have lately become very keen to defend those parts of their culture which they see as essentially Spanish, as defining a unique and well-defended home, something inherited with Spanish *sangre*: born in the blood.

Naturally, I dreamed of bulls. For this night and all of the others in my trip, I dreamed of bulls. They sneaked in under every other thought and I let them—they make a good obsession, something solid to drive out less pleasant images. Too many empty hotel rooms can cause depression—if you still count a room as empty with me inside it, which, of course, I do. So the more bulls, the merrier—bring them all in.

The first bull I met belonged to the farmer father of a school friend. It stood, largely motionless, in its own small field: a solid block of threat, massive as a camper van, legs hidden almost to the hooves by slabs and folds of flesh. At the relevant time of year, it would sport an infernal erection and slowly, dreadfully swivel its head and roar for sex. Teenage girl that I was, it stuck in my mind: the glistening of its muzzle, the gargantuan clouds of its breath, its absolute animality.

And this would have been a good bull to dream of, a homely bull, an almost friendly thing to start off the list of bull faces, bull stories, bull facts, the wilful mesh and clutter of research which, for safety's sake, I'm always very happy to have with me, swilling about behind my eyes.

But, in fact, I can't remember which particular bully forms trotted out and wandered my head on that particular bully night, so I'll write you a compound of *Bulls in General*, a summation of my daytime studies and their night-time fruits.

We'll begin with that first bull, a domestic animal, which is to say that it was probably three times the weight of an average toro bravo and had a conformation and temperament very different from anything bred for the corrida. But even a modern, humdrum, farmyard bull has an unusual status among livestock. It is domesticated and useful, but also monstrous and unpredictable. Not so long ago a man was gored to death at the roadside by an Ayrshire bull that simply burst through its fence and repeatedly attacked him. The man had been taking water samples beside the field and, said witnesses, had offered the animal no provocation. I know of a farmer who liked walking ahead of his bull whenever he moved it. For years, they ambled together past their respective neighbours, a model of mastered nature and justified trust. Then one day, without warning, the animal butted its owner in the back and broke his spine. My first bull, I'm sure, had the strength to break a spine. But perhaps the thought to do so never actually entered its head. It could never dream, as I can, of a man's body, lifted by an animal into the air, limbs already forced into shapes against their nature.

As a human being, I can have very little idea of what thoughts and images, if any, *do* enter a bull's head. I have read description after description of corridas where bulls are described as "brave," as "wise," as "cowardly": where they are portrayed as lowering their heads in supplication to the matador before the kill, and all but asking in polite Castilian for their own deaths. And a number of writers have kindly informed me of precisely what a toro is thinking at any given time. Barnaby Conrad in *Death of a Matador* has assured me that a toro's breeding told it, on its entry into the ring, that "it was here to fight and kill."* Many of these same writers have criticised opponents of the corrida for anthropomorphising the bulls, for endowing them with a human sensibility.

For my part, the bulls I dream of are blurry, perhaps caught in the midst of motion, and show no sign of consciousness. And I realise that we often see our world, our companions, our animals, as we wish them, or need them to be. Where one party witnesses suffering in the corrida, another finds willing participation and bravery. Invalided out of my first evening in Spain and, so far, only familiar with the corrida on TV and film, in scattered narratives and photographs, I simply lay and stared up at the darkened ceiling—a former writer with no words for the bulls.

And let's say the ache in my neck meant that I slept lightly, because this is true. And let's suggest that the uneasy press of the pillow was, on that night, overlaid with the dunt of another bovine apparition, capering there in the back of my skull. And we've already passed midnight, we're in the time when even the simplest image—that of the jet-black, cartoon bull—is no longer simple.

I've watched so many videos of toros in the ring that

---

*Written by a former torero, *Death of a Matador* is a highly atmospheric, fictionalised account of a bullfighter's final hours, interlarded with technically accurate but often hyperbolic descriptions of the corrida.

I recognise the patterns of movement and form the cartoons exaggerate. The *toro de lidia** does indeed have those intensely muscular forequarters the drawings parody, and its body does then taper away to a slimmish waist and lower-slung, slighter back legs. Its weight is concentrated where it can do the most damage and absorb the greatest impact. When the toro turns, its hindquarters do sometimes seem to bicycle away almost independently at the far end of a visibly inflexible spine and it does toss its head. It may snort, or bellow, and may even paw the ground, although this is taken to be a sign of extreme unease rather than threat. This said, the threat beyond the cartoon silhouette is real; the toro—hampered by its build and the unwieldy presence of its considerable testicles—may have a fairly poor turning circle, but it also has remarkable, explosive energy. Over short, straight distances, it can keep pace with a race horse and (arguments about modern, feeble strains aside) it is bred to be inclined to charge.

And if I'm going to consider breeding, I'll now have to note that the ancestor of the modern toro bravo is said to be an even more terrifying animal: the completely and genuinely feral, ancient European bison—the aurochs, or to be more technical, *Bos primigenius.* Up to six feet high at the shoulder, long-headed and ferociously horned, they have earned their place in the Palaeolithic cave paintings of—among other places—Altamira in Spain. There, they were depicted by the people who possibly hunted and possibly worshipped

*Another name for *toro bravo.* Literally bull of the struggle.

them and who used pigments mixed with animal blood to paint the signature lines and curves that make the unmistakable shape of a bull and mark a point where art and sympathetic magic meet, where survival and faith can conjoin. The American matador John Fulton took his lead from Altamira to make his own paintings, naturally using pigments suspended in bull's blood, sometimes the blood of bulls he had killed in the corrida—a ritual with a trinity of acts within which faith and survival can conjoin.

Now there are no more aurochs. The monster cattle with monster horns that hooked and charged to defend their herds and young, the probable scourge of Palaeolithic man, died out in the wild in the Polish forests of the late seventeenth century. The last animal in captivity, property of the King of Prussia, died in 1712 in his Berlin zoo.

When I imagine aurochs, they have the same solemnly patient expression that seems to haunt the great auk, the dodo, the giant sloth. The portraits of extinct species always seem to endow them with an entirely human and urgent awareness of their own mortality.

I can, with very little effort, set my fictional aurochs charging, like huge depressives across the sleepless night: I can have them chase the flick and tease of red cloths in Vespasian's Colosseum. Julius Caesar introduced these ferocious fighting bulls to the arena in one of the many imperial attempts to satisfy the Roman public's need for novelty. The bulls were fought over sand on foot by pig-tailed gladiators who were armed with swords and crimson lures. The echoes of the corrida are almost too obvious.

As it happens, I know the Colosseum a little. I learned the seating plan of Roman arenas at school in Latin lessons, could name the parts of the gladiators' unforgiving accoutrements and could recite *Morituri te Salutant* before I understood the complexities of its grammar, or the available shades in its translation. *Those who are about to die salute* you can just as easily be rendered as *those who are going to die salute you.* In the first case, the gladiators speak for themselves and their awareness of their imminent danger: in the second case they speak for anyone alive.

When I had work to do in Rome—the travelling writer again—I spent part of my one day off in the Colosseum. The arena floor is missing and the circuit of the upper structure is now incomplete, but the monument is still impressive. It is also surprisingly repulsive. Sitting in heat amplified to a stinging pitch by the curves of so much naked stone and years before I came to write this book, I wondered if the negative atmosphere of the place was real or simply my projection. A helicopter clattered overhead and the noise of its rotors, trapped in the albeit incomplete drum of the walls, caught and thundered, touched me in the ribs like a ghost of the crowds that used to roar and stamp here, watching the spill of human and animal blood. In the darker passageways, the stairwells, I found the sense of something humid, vicious, sleazy. The arena itself stank of old threat, felt hungry for overkill.

At that time, I'd already heard the stories of men, inflamed by an afternoon of carnage in Rome's more decadent days, rushing in a kind of blood trance to the ranks of waiting prostitutes outside the building. And in those decadent days, when common or garden blood-shed was not enough and a desensitised and demanding audience had to be pricked into appreciation with ever more elaborate displays, I'm told that the legend of Pasiphaë was re-enacted in the Colosseum.

Pasiphaë, you may remember, was the wife of Minos, King of Crete. Minos' mother was Europa, a woman seduced by Zeus while he took on the form of a bull. Which makes Minos a combination of the bovine, human and divine which you'll find is not uncommon in myths—should you start searching for bulls in myths. Pasiphaë, already married to an almost-bull, then fell in love with an *actual* bull and had the ingenious Daedalus build her a cow costume so that she could consummate her new passion. The result of this union was the Mino-taur—a shameful freak, far too obviously both bull and man—who was confined to the labyrinth Daedalus de-signed to hold him. There Theseus, the matador and murderer, killed him.

I will also mention that Italy takes its name from "land of bulls" and that Europe takes its name from Europa, wife, lover and mother of bulls. Europe is full of more or less quaint and resonant fertility stories con-cerned with more or less magical and divine bulls. The spectacle and repercussions of a woman actually being mounted by a bull for the benefit of a jaded mob, I will leave you to imagine for yourself.

And back in my hotel—you remember my hotel?—perhaps all the street noise had faded away to indicate that even night-owl Madrid had gone to bed. And perhaps it was time, before the autumn dawn, to roll out what I know of the pantheon of bulls: the sacred cattle, the dreams of thousands, the dreams which, it could be argued, have stuck in our blood.

I'll name the bull god Anu who sends a bull from heaven to fight with Gilgamesh in the Babylonian *Epic of Gilgamesh*. Then there are the ancient bull gods of Sumeria and Mesopotamia. In pre-dynastic Egypt and all across North Africa, cattle were honoured and worshipped. One of Ancient Egypt's earliest divinities was the cow-headed fertility goddess, Hathor, who consumed the sun each night and released him each morning, dyeing the horizon red with the blood of childbirth. In India, of course, cattle remain sacred to Hindus—in one of their multiplicity of interlacing cosmic views, our whole world is balanced on the back of a sacred cow. Meanwhile, the Plains Indians treasure the buffalo and the Masai still trouble themselves to be the official owners of all cattle in the world.

The bull cult in Crete left us with the Minotaur and his unhappy fate, the sacred maze and the sacrifical axe that both bear the name labyrinth and the bull dancers depicted leaping over bulls in the Knossos murals. I remember tracing out the unlikely lines of their limbs and horns when I was a schoolgirl. Ancient depictions of similar bull dancers and a similar maze design have now been found in Egypt.

Ancient Egypt, the land of Hathor, was also the kingdom of the Apis bulls: bull after bull in a line of bovine succession which reached from the Early to the Late Dynasty. The Apis bull was a god in both life and death.

A black bull with a distinctive white marking, he was recognised, picked out and then pampered as the person-ification of Ptah, the creator god of Memphis. The very water that washed his hide was precious. Having reached his entirely natural death each bull was carefully mum-mified and then represented Osiris, god of the dead.

In the time of Ptolemy I the cult of Serapis emerged, a synthetic religion, based partly on the Apis cult and designed to appeal to both Greeks and Egyptians. The Serapic cult is thought to have influenced and been influenced by Zoroastrianism, Judaism, Hinduism and ultimately the newly emerging Christianity.

Meanwhile, the bull-focused religion of Mithraism had developed in the Roman Empire and was officially adopted in the time of Pompey. Mithra was an Aryan god of light who conquered a bull god and released a veritable cornucopia when he spilt its blood. Temples were erected to Mithra, where he was worshipped using the sacrifice of bulls. The Roman arena at Merida in Spain is still used for corridas today and, it so happens, is built on an even more ancient site of bull sacrifice. For thousands of years, bull's blood has been shed on that same ground.

So consider Spain, just before Christianity's first cen-tury. The country was already awash with bull folk tales and practices. To the South there were the African bull cults; to the North there were the Celts with their horned gods; to the East were Egypt, Greece and Rome: all with bull-worshipping cultures. Spain was hemmed in by sacred cattle and salt water, by ideas of bloodshed, death and rebirth. It's hardly surprising that Spain embraced first the blood and life of the bull cults, and then the blood and life of Christianity with a passion sufficient to spark and sustain the most florid manifestation of the Inquisition. It's equally unsurprising that early Christianity took over the feast days of Mithraism and made the horns, the cloven hooves and the frank sexuality of the bull the identifying characteristics of Satan. And it will also be no shock that, later, Pope Pius V, worried by a bull-besotted Spain, promised excommunication for anyone taking part in a corrida and that, in 1558—excommunication having failed to impress— Pope Sixtus V tried to ban at least the clergy from attending. This move also foundered amid howls of protest against such an insult to Spanish blood.

But if this is all too far away and long ago, I can consider the bulls sacrificed by the Gaels to Shoney the sea god. Or seventeenth-century Scotland, where bulls were buried alive to let witchcraft bring fertility to the land and herds. Contemporary voodoo can boast a number of bull *loa*, and a contemporary practice of bull sacrifice. This book is published by an imprint with offices in London, the city of Bull Markets, the city where the early street plan followed the spatter of blood from a ritually wounded bull.

Or else I can think of my mother, years before I was born, visiting the Birmingham museum (Birmingham, city of the bull ring) and watching a demonstration of the new machine used to oxygenate human blood during the earliest heart transplant procedures. The machine, she told me, was tested using bovine blood and I have always chosen to believe her.

The power and the danger, the lines of inheritance and the human need for risk, they're all in the blood—the useful, heated liquid that clumps past my ears in the close dark of each night. And behind the blood-coloured shade of my eyelids I can dream of the blood shed in slaughter for meat, or spilled for sacrifice, the blood given meaning beyond itself. There's more than a scent of that about the corrida—the potency of blood in a Christian context and in an earlier, pagan ritual. The fear behind much of the writing against the corrida seems to be that something pagan happens in the arena which turns human nature towards the bestial, the orgiastic, the uncontrolled: the darkness of chaos and of blood.

Among the supporters of the corrida there are often expressions of intense respect for the bull. This is the kind of respect which, in humans, will often demand an animal's death. To ritually extinguish the life of a sacred animal, or to hold it inviolate—in time after time and place after place human cultures choose between these two courses of action: these two different expressions of love.

I woke up stiff and vaguely nauseous on my first morning in Spain. Outside the streets were leaden with gusty rain and the cold tensed my shoulders into spasm. I negotiated the moderately cosy subway to reach Puerta del Sol and look for Calle Victoria and the advance ticket office for the Plaza de Toros Monumental. The damp commuters around me appeared to be as miserable as I felt.

My route took me past a doorway guarded by two Guardia Civil: two men in the familiar uniforms, the sinister-laughable black leather hats. Ten years in the West of Scotland have filled me with stories of the Civil War, the Scottish Republican volunteers, the evils of the Guardia Civil. Although these two particular men may have been no more or less morally compromised than any pair of policemen, I watched them as if they were werewolves, something not human at all, concerned only with power and bloodshed, the usual elements of fascist ritual. The doorway that sheltered them from the rain leads to government offices now, but in Franco's time the building was a political prison. Its personnel and their diligent labours earned the place a charming nom de guerre—the House of Screams.

The tiny corrida ticket office was, when I reached it, closed and would be until Friday, but I stood for a while and watched water pearling down the blaze of posters that surrounded its grey metal shutters. Layers of paper and paste had given the walls the look of something organic, but over the uneven surface shone the newest layer of swirling capes and thundering bulls, towering portraits in the colours of circus posters with text that promised the finest bulls, the most dazzling toreros, the most perfect fiesta. I read that in a week or so Christina Sánchez, the best of the female toreros (she prefers to be known as a torero, not a torera), would fight in a ring near Madrid on an all-female *cartel.** And on Sunday,

---

*The poster or bill used to advertise a corrida, or, more loosely, the list of toreros involved in a particular corrida, whose names would be shown on the *cartel.*

three *novilleros*—apprentice matadors—would fight at Las Ventas, the Madrid Plaza de Toros Monumental. I would be in Madrid on Sunday.

So it was decided—the first corrida I saw was to be a *novillada*—an apprentice fiesta. I was inadvertently following Hemingway's advice and beginning with an untrained observation of the inexperienced. Hemingway, the writer who found his voice in Spain with the bulls.

And this was where all of those bull gods brought me, to a wet side street, peppered with aficionado bars, in a strange city with a bitter history. I straggled across the road and tried to discuss the corrida in my terrible Spanish with a man selling lottery tickets from a little kiosk. He broke the first smile I'd seen in Madrid that day—I'd made him happy by complimenting something he was proud of in his culture, taking an interest in something Spanish, something in the blood.

Chapter Three

Three Bad Days

15:45. My first afternoon in Spain and I'm leaving from Madrid's Atocha Station on a south-bound train. This seems slightly surprising—my Spanish travel vocabulary is just patchy enough to have bought me the wrong kind of ticket and then sent me off to an unpremeditated destination. But, unusually, it turns out that I'm exactly where I should be, at exactly the right time, committed to a six-hour journey by a sentimental impulse.

I'm heading for Granada, a picturesque little place, distinguished by its concentrations of various guitar-related skills, by an opera involving cigars and toreadors, the Alhambra paradise gardens and other remnants of a Moorish past. And, of course, in a land fond of sacrifice, Granada has a famously martyred son: the poet and playwright Federico García Lorca, killed in 1936 by Nationalists, during the opening days of the Civil War. Lorca, a writer who died because of his art, because of his politics, because of his sexuality, because he had put himself in altogether the wrong place at entirely the wrong time. His murder satisfied the petty jealousies that might be found in any town, the type of half-shamed, half-righteous sadism that rarely fails to thrive under the absolution of a killing time.

Lorca grew up in Granada in the first decades of our century. Like any young artist worth his salt, he left home for the capital, in this case cosmopolitan, permissive Madrid, and took mind-expanding trips to pacy New York and racy Cuba. But he always came back to his family and to the town he loved for its tolerant, artistic, non-Christian traditions and hated for its small-minded, viciously provincial bourgeoisie. A man obsessed by death and quite literally unable to run, a Leftist figurehead who had just made a press attack on the Granadino middle class, Lorca made one last visit to Granada precisely when he shouldn't—during the opening, bloody confusion of what was becoming a particularly dirty war.

On the night of 13th July 1936, against all advice, Lorca left Madrid and safety and caught the sleeper train to Granada from Atocha Station. For a few turbulent weeks, he stayed relatively safe, though frightened, in his home town. Then, on 16th August, Lorca was arrested while hiding at a friend's house in the Calle de Angulo and was taken away as "a Russian spy." Two or perhaps three days later, he was executed by a Nationalist death squad: dead at thirty-eight, his body abandoned in a gully in the hills beyond the town, a couple of extra bullets in his arse, just to show that certain fascist flair for symbolism. A left-wing teacher died beside him along with two minor toreros, both anarchists.

Alive and free to write in 1998, I watch while the platform drags and drops beside the window, flattens to nothing as we put on speed. And, of course, I think of Lorca's voice, its future stolen, the eloquence of his life removed by the standard totalitarian means. And, of course, I also think that if I had any backbone I would write as best I can, simply because I can, because of the silenced dead, because writing is a privilege and also a responsibility. But, then, as I've pointed out, my backbone doesn't work.

So I avoid the issue by unearthing biographical parallels, playing *compare and contrast*. Lorca was, for example, an unhappy writer who spent much of his life contemplating the horrors, the fascinations and the strengths of death. He tended to love attractive but damaging men. His faith was sometimes overwhelming, sometimes desolate, often overshadowed with confusion and guilt—no room for God's love if you hate yourself. He adored the theatre, acted a little, believed in the strength of words let loose, out loud. This last point I find a particular comfort—I've suspended my belief in words, but I'm happy to be close to his. Even after all this time, I still look for company in words, I still want to believe in the possibilities of inspiration.

And I'm happy to have Lorca in mind for this journey, because he admired the corrida, because that was one of his inspirations and because he was my way in to the corrida. The Hemingway bravado did nothing for me: the menopausal bar-room stories, the foreigner trying too hard to be part of Spain, but, all the while, hoping to keep it exclusive, defining the country, for the first time, as one vast DT-haunted tourist club. Not that *compare and contrast* again—Papa Hemingway is keeping entirely out of the picture. Like Juan Belmonte, the great torero, Papa killed himself at the end of his career. And Papa came to Spain, a young man, and found out that he could write and then came back, much older, and proved that he couldn't anymore, that he'd made it go away. I don't want to think what I'll prove while I'm here.

So I'll think about Lorca instead. Lorca, whose imagination returned again and again to the image of Saint Sebastian: a man martyred, much as the bull is—and much as the torero can be—by multiple, public penetrations. Lorca, who followed the corrida and who, in his youth, even had himself carried through the streets of Granada, costumed and bloodied as if he were a matador who had received a fatal *cornada*.* (This being only one of his many exorcisms of his own death.) He was a friend of Ignacio Sánchez Mejías, a gentle-eyed, polymath, bisexual and wholly reckless killer of bulls. After Mejías' death in the ring, Lorca wrote a poem in his memory.† And Lorca famously redefined and explored the word *duende*—an item of vocabulary indispensable to any understanding of the aficionado's passion for the corrida.

Look it up in a Spanish dictionary and you will find *duende* given as *goblin, imp, malign spirit* or perhaps *poltergeist*—it also carries apparently contradictory suggestions of being granted contact with either an earth spirit or a higher self. For Lorca, the word became a short-

---

*The term for all but the most glancing penetration by a bull's horn.
†"Lament for Ignacio Sánchez Mejías," published in 1935.

hand for the source of any piece of art with "dark notes." It represented a transcendent, but melancholy, moment conjured up by work with roots in a painful inspiration, a loss, a sacrifice. Duende was not an evil genius, but a sad one. For him it was perhaps the price that Catholic guilt demanded for a life given over to acts of intellectual, rather than divine, creation, or else an obligation to give private and public suffering a voice.

Lorca, although a great internationalist, believed that duende was most at home in Spain. He felt that duende's atmosphere, its adoration and immortalisation of the dead were all deeply Spanish. He saw duende's power at work particularly strongly in the *cante jondo*—the "deep songs" of flamenco music, so called because they were intended to be sung from the depths of the Andalucian soul. He also saw duende in certain passages of certain corridas—the corrida also being something said to sing, deep in the Andalucian soul. When a lecturer first talked to me about duende at university, I knew—with an entirely uncharacteristic spasm of student interest—that it was something I wanted, something for which I already had an appetite, something which words could create. I didn't know then that, when aficionados talk about great corridas, they seem always to describe uncovered moments of duende, of sad, numinous beauty.

Some critics (and aficionados) dismiss duende as the product of self-aggrandising gypsy hocum, or as a simple reflection of Lorca's personal griefs: his life as a self-loathing sensualist, an incautious but easily damaged artist, a homosexual in conservative, Catholic Spain. Although I'm alternately bored and frustrated by the

standard model of the artist as a tortured soul too sensitive to live—or at least too sensitive to be lived *with*—I
would still argue that a concept like duende has its uses.
It can be a reminder that destruction does have an inti-
mate relationship with creativity, even if it is simply the
destruction of the empty space which precedes it, or the
necessary removal of the earlier, poorer forms that lead
to a finished piece of work. It can act as a description of
the "soul" which offers itself beautifully, and cruelly, to
specific human beings at specific moments—but try to
trap it, guarantee it, take it for granted and it melts away.

But, right now, as the train smoothes and sways
through the dog end of the suburbs, duende isn't any-
where near the forefront of my mind. For reasons I can't
imagine but would like to circumvent, I can only think
of Lorca's remarkable gift with photographs. Even in
casual snapshots he seems to present something of his
nature almost as fully as he might in words. Alone, or in
groups of less well-aware faces, Lorca looks out. Your
eyes meet his and see what he's made of himself for only
you: the trademark, solidly black widow's peak, the
slightly teasing, slightly childlike, slightly vulnerable
eyes and the mouth: sometimes pensive, shy, delighted,
but always extremely, almost accusingly, alive.

And, of course, in his images Lorca can't help but
have that overshadowed air, that hint of prefigured
extinction. In some pictures, he might almost be aware
of the darkness coming, might almost be asking himself
when it will come, when a man who loves his country
will be killed by other men who love it differently. He
only seems wholly free of his ghost in pictures taken

while he's performing. In front of an audience, the champion of duende seems entirely unself-conscious and entirely happy at his work. This is a phenomenon often described by artistic and sporting performers, and by writers and toreros, too—this is the time when the self deserts you and the joy slips in. It grants an access to self-forgetting without self-destruction, and it's a moment that can seem worth almost any price, even the torero's ultimate risk. This selfless place, this energetic peace, may also be all the performer recalls of something observers might well define as duende.

This afternoon, unfortunately, I'm leaving the city, but not myself, behind: no duende here. Passing a tall, white graffiti slogan which even I can translate as *Spain for the Spanish*, I sit on one of the unforgiving bench seats of my carriage and realise that the effort of getting my bags and myself from the hotel to the station to the platform and then here has left me with hands that are shaking quite uncontrollably. Opposite me sits a Spanish matron who tells me she is also travelling to Granada and then going further yet in a car which will be driven by, I think, a relative—I don't know what brand of relative, I don't recognise the word. She is clearly unimpressed by my shoddy pronunciation of her language, by my shaking, by my thin but permanent veneer of sweat. I, on the other hand, am becoming used to myself as one of the Sisterhood of the Legally Medicated—I feel that perhaps this is now the way I will always be. I try to think of the most comfortable position for my head and decide it would travel best as a separate item, in a box on the luggage rack.

Meanwhile, the seats around me are taken up by a scatter of repulsively healthy back-packers and several highly ornate but stern-featured nuns. After a dash or two of desultory small talk, we all fall silent. A conductor arrives with headphones for those who wish to hear the dubbed Steven Seagal movie showing on the tiny screens bolted high in the far corners of the carriage. I decline his offer—wouldn't understand the soundtrack and I can't turn my head enough to face either of the screens. Instead I watch the dry plain spinning smoothly out around us, the silvered leaves of distant olive groves shifting against an unheard breeze like one vast vegetable pelt. Then I take another one of my pain killers and try to read about bulls—the undomesticated, bred for the ring, *toros bravos* (this isn't taken literally by the Spanish but does mean *brave bulls*) or *toros de lidia* (very roughly, bulls of the corrida) or (should you want it in Latin) bulls of the species *Bos taurus ibericus*.

To begin, never mind that Hemingway will tell you a *toro bravo* is an Exocet on hooves, a psychopathic creature likely to break into houses and gore grandmothers by their own hearths. This is not the case. It is true, however, that the *toro bravo* has been bred to highlight certain elements of standard bovine behaviour, particularly *agresividad*—aggression.

Now cattle—even *toros bravos*—are at their most docile and content in groups. They are herd animals and this means that one of their defence strategies is to stick with the crowd, sharing out a reduced risk of predation and gaining the benefit of many other watchfully nervous herbivores as an early warning system. For a herd animal, isolation means death and if that sets a little chill in your spine also, remember that apes and humans are group animals, too. That solitude is fatal is both literal and instinctive truth for the toro bravo which will die alone in the ring and which can be transported most easily from place to place when snugly surrounded by a herd of steers, should it happen to like the look of the steers.

So far so good. But, unlike the gazelle and many other endearingly defenceless prey species, cattle, bison and buffalo (or even, for the sake of argument, gnus) are armed with horns, an explosive turn of speed and impressive weight and power. This means that they can defend themselves, their group and their young against predators. Equine species may lash out at pursuers, but the bovines take things one stage further—their response to many types of threat is to charge at it. They run away, forwards.

Add to this the fact that cattle are highly stimulated by certain types of movement—surreally, these are roughly the same flicking, teasing movements which entice a kitten into charging—and you have an animal which has an instinctive predisposition to charge when placed alone in an alien arena and drawn on by dancing capes. You will already have worked out that, by this reckoning, the bull which charges hardest and looks the bravest may actually be the most stressed and fearful. So *agresividad* might be translated by a realist as *terror*, or *extreme stress*.

You may wish to learn that another well-armed herbivore, the rhinoceros, exhibits similar responses. According to his autobiography, Juan Belmonte induced just such a beast to respond to passes with the cape in pretty much the manner of a toro bravo. This was, of course, intended as a light-hearted demonstration of Belmonte's skills, rather than an experiment in animal behaviour, and did not lead to the rhino's death or injury, as far as I know. The incident also did not lead to any calls for a rhinoceros corrida, although I will mention that I've seen a photograph of the metal cage and the toro involved in a bull versus tiger fight in the Madrid Plaza at the end of the nineteenth century when the corrida was not quite the purist affair that some aficionados would have you believe. I'm told the tiger lost.

Rhinos and tigers aside, the corrida is, at one very basic level, an attempt to control and exploit the known behaviours of the bull. But I've already mentioned that the toro bravo is a bull developed over time to have *casta*: the fighting spirit necessary for the corrida, an exaggeration of its "fight in flight" programming. The beginnings of this breeding process are difficult to trace.

Although there is general agreement that there's a good deal of aurochs about a toro bravo, no one has much of an idea—beyond the obvious—of how those traces got there. It's believed that the forebears of the present-day toro bravo were African aurochs brought to Spain by the Carthaginians, who were not unacquainted with bull-worshipping Romans, and by the Berbers, who were not unacquainted with the bull-worshipping Egyptians and who were bull worshippers themselves. These vaguely domesticated bison, the theories go, may well have broken loose here and there, slipped back into their old ways and made a terrifying and admirable spectacle, while breeding with European aurochs. At some point in the eleventh century A.D., if not before, the fighting potential of the bulls was recognised and the first experiments in the corrida, and a whole range of other bull-related, but not overtly religious, risk-taking began.

In the sixteenth century there were already recognised bull breeders, and by the beginning of the seventeenth century there are records of the first known separate strain of toro bravo, the Jijona—a reportedly fierce type of animal, roughly the same colour as an Irish setter. By the eighteenth century, facts are far easier to come by and we see the creation in Andalucia of the four strains of toro bravo from which all modern Spanish stock derives: the Raíz Cabrera, the Raíz Gallardo, the Raíz Vázquez and the famous Raíz Vistahermosa.

The names of modern strains like the Vizconde de Rosembuj, the Duque de Antxobez, or the Marqués de Nagore betray the gentility of many bull breeders, or ganaderos. For this reason, many bull bloodlines were destroyed during the Civil War by the democratic, and hungry, fury of the anti-fascist forces. Juan Belmonte himself was confronted by gentlemen of the Left, anxious to relieve him of the toros he had amassed in semi-retiral. At which point, he was recognised and acknowledged as a matador, risen from a poor family, who had earned his money, and therefore his bulls, by his own efforts in the ring. This earned his cattle a stay of execution. Developing a bloodline would be the torero equivalent of a footballer opening a pub.

(Although some toreros, more anxious for contact with the public than with toros, do open pubs.) Hemingway's darling matador, Antonio Ordóñez, became a ganadero, as did the great Domingo Ortega, whom Hemingway professed to hate. One of Domingo's bulls was responsible for the first fatality in the Las Ventas ring—goring Félix Almagro González in the neck. How a matador must feel when one of his bulls kills another torero, I can't begin to imagine.

Among all modern bulls, the Miura strain still has the most ominous reputation for providing man-killers—a reputation based on fact. In their 150-year history, Miuras have killed more toreros than any other bull. It was a Miura bull, called "Islero," that killed the great torero "Manolete" on 28th August 1947 and I have seen the mounted head—the impressively massive and generously horned head—of his mother, "Islera," who was killed soon after, as is customary, to prevent her breeding any further homicides. Miuras have killed no one since "Manolete," perhaps in part because, balancing honour against self-preservation, so many first-rate matadors refuse to fight Miuras and they have fallen out of high-profile use. Miuras may also have been bred to be a little calmer, of late. Nevertheless, the Miura name remains synonymous with ultimate risk, possibly as a mark of respect from a culture so much in love with tradition and "brave" toros. Currently the bulls of Victorino Martín are almost undoubtedly this generation's most hazardous toros.

And this is where the individual bloodline of bulls becomes more than a matter for arcane aficionado discussion. A torero contracts to fight bulls from a particular source each time he enters the ring. This means that he may, if he has sufficient standing, avoid contracting Miuras or other troublesome bulls. Equally, he can pick bulls with which he knows he has a chance of performing well. If he is a person of any experience, he will have learned the details of habit that each strain exhibits. To keep himself alive, he will have studied not just the minutiae of general bull behaviour, but also the tricks and idiosyncrasies of each breed.

Naturally, with the passage of time, strains have risen, fallen and disappeared. The overall picture given by many aficionados is often that bulls in a variety of past Golden Ages were monstrous while those creeping about today are only half a ton of *docilidad*. Although today's bull may be more lacking in casta and less threatening to a matador's life and career, their safety is relative—they still can, and do, kill. The glorious bulls of old are referred to as "mastodons" or "cathedrals" who could only be defeated by Olympian heroes. One such was Pedro Romero, the first man to be called "the father of the modern corrida." He fought between 1771 and 1799, and is said to have killed 5,600 bulls without receiving any kind of injury. He founded the Rodeño school of *toreo*—the art or craft of playing bulls in the corrida. Based around the town of Ronda, this brand of toreo is said to reflect a melancholy, dignified approach to the corrida and a certain manifest respect for the bull. Other styles would include the more frankly macho, improvisational Madrileño school and the upbeat, flamboyant Sevillian.

Whatever the faults of modern bulls—and we will deal with many of them later—they can be seen as exhibiting a fairly standard range of character. Some bulls may charge easily (*celoso*—an eager bull, or *codicioso*—a bull hungry for action) and in a predictable, straight line which makes them safer for toreros to work. They may be *manso* (which would translate either as *cowardly* or *stressed into defensive inaction*) and may refuse to charge, may charge erratically, or simply hook their heads which can make them immensely dangerous and unpredictable. I have seen film of toros mansos leaping the *barrera*, the high wooden wall around the arena, and invading the corridor behind it in either a misguided bid for freedom or a stress reaction to the rigours of the corrida and perhaps the presence of the crowd. I have seen bulls refuse to move from the gate, the *toril*, through which they've entered and run from the picador and his lance, instead of making the hoped-for charges towards him.

It is up to the matador and his cuadrilla to control bulls of whatever temperament, unless they are actually declared unfit by the observing president and/or loudly protesting crowd. A fine matador proves himself such by working both with and against the bull's instincts in order to produce tempered movements, an interaction where the bull appears to be *fijado*, or *fixed*, with its total attention on the lure and not the man.

The knowledge that the bull can be fooled into targeting a cape and not the man manipulating it is, of course, central to toreo and the chances of any matador's survival. The strenuous efforts made to keep the form and actions of an unmounted human being unfamiliar to the toro bravo brings us to the *ganaderías*, the ranches on which the bulls are kept, roaming almost entirely as they would in the wild.

I've seen film and photographs of the toros bravos at home on their ranges, idling under trees, drinking with their forelegs deep in silky, grass-fringed pools, or silhouetted impressively on rural horizons, living the good and moderately feral life. And it is a pretty good life at the ganadería. A calf, once it has suffered one bad day, filled with the shocks of branding, ear notching and inoculation, is given its own name and left much to its own devices for three, or even as many as six, years, although toreros would much rather not fight a bull with six years of experience behind it. It's in the pastures of the ganadería that the toros bravos become accustomed to the adult length of their horns and learn to butt, toss and hook with them in tussles with each other. A bull of four or five years entering the ring will still have a good idea of how to handle itself—although very little idea of how to deal with a good torero.

The second bad day comes with the *tienta*. As I've mentioned, it is believed that the casta—the fighting spirit—of a bull is inherited from the cow while the *trapío*—the physical conformation—is inherited from the father. Each stud bull is given a harem of twenty or so selected cows. These cows are tested at two years old in proceedings called *tientas*. During a tienta, the cow will be placed in a small ring and faced by a mounted *vaquero*—the Spanish, and quite frankly far more stylish, equivalent of a cowboy—who is armed with a vara—a lance—and acts as a picador. If the cow charges the horse and keeps coming, despite being lightly wounded by the lance, this is a sign of good breeding potential. The cow will also be played with the cape by a torero who may be an old hand getting in some practice with the faster-turning female of the species, or a lucky newcomer, trying to impress, or even a particularly reckless aficionado, keen to try the cape. Some tientas are semi-public auditions for torero and beast alike and some are strictly closed affairs. If the cow passes her test, she will be classified *brava* and kept on for breeding, if she hasn't shown sufficient spirit she will be classed as *buey*, or *beef*, for obvious reasons. Two-year-old bulls who may be used for stud are tested using only the picador.

The young toros are also tested and those which fail will also go for beef, as will—for that matter—those who die in the ring. Some bulls intended for the ring are tried for spirit, in a process known as *acoso y derribo—chase and knock down*. This is now only used in more traditional ranches and was a favourite pastime of Juan Belmonte. It involves chasing a bull on horseback, while armed with a stout wooden staff. This staff is used to tip the bull over by exerting pressure on his hindquarters once he has been set slightly off balance—I don't see the attraction myself, but it's apparently addictive for those so inclined. All young bulls meet a picador before they go to the corrida and are assessed on their keenness to attack before and after being injured. This first exposure to a man with a lance may well explain what appears to be the toro's instinctive dislike of picadors in the ring—

the bull has met this challenge before and is usually keen
to charge at it.

The bulls for the ring are never played with the
cape—although some bulls appear in the plaza with a
knowing air which suggests that they may at some time
have met something like a matador, perhaps in an informal *capea*,* perhaps when a would-be torero has sneaked
out into the field and tried a few passes with them. But
every effort is made to keep each toro de lidia away from
dismounted men. Mounted vaqueros move the animals
whenever necessary, armed with long wooden staffs to
defend themselves and surrounding the bulls with steers
to keep them docile. This, in theory, prevents a bull
from developing *sentido*, the potentially fatal knowledge
that the man in the ring is his enemy and not the cloth.
The toro should only have the fifteen or so minutes of
the corrida to begin and complete his education—even
so, some alert animals who genuinely haven't been in
any kind of arena before do develop this awareness
frighteningly fast, the Miura bulls being the most notorious for sentido. But at this point it must be said that
bulls are not especially intelligent—they are dangerous
and sometimes cunning, but not bright. As I once heard
a old-time cowboy say—"You'll never see a cow in a circus, doing tricks. They're dumb."

But, as I've mentioned, some toros do have extra
lessons in toreo. Aspiring toreros have been known to
steal into the jealously guarded fields of the ganaderías

---

*An informal, illegal and often chaotic village square event, where some-
times bulls, sometimes cows and sometimes quite experienced and therefore dangerous animals are played by occasionally massive crowds of
amateurs.

under cover of darkness to practise playing the toros. If they're acting responsibly, they will pick out cows to play, but they may still inadvertently expose the bulls to the mysteries of the cape and its master. Sophisticated efforts are made to prevent this happening, but it has not been unknown for the particularly foolhardy and obsessed to slip through the net. Most notably, Juan Belmonte told lyrical tales of his repeated excursions to the ganaderías near his home in Seville. He and his friends would swim across the river to the pastures, leaving their clothes on the far bank, and then set off, completely naked, to corner and attempt to cape a cow. Many aficionados have begun their love affair with the corrida by reading Belmonte's descriptions of playing toros by moonlight, of feeling the rough heat of the animal's body thunder past his naked skin. He even tried to cape a bull in total darkness, relying only on a kind of masochistic love of toreo and a growing faith in his instinctive knowledge of toros' reactions which would ultimately allow him to work bulls in the ring, closer to his body than ever before.

And here I will mention Civilón, a bull with very peculiar reactions—a bull who almost did tricks: one trick, anyway. Fed by hand and carefully tamed by a ranch hand on a ganadería near Salamanca, Civilón became famous as a placid toro de lidia—one who could be safely surrounded by frolicking children, even when he was isolated from the herd. Predictably, in 1936, the management of the Barcelona plaza booked the by then famous Civilón to take part in a corrida with "El Estudiante," a torero called Luis Gómez Calleja. This might, quite reasonably, be expected to have been the end of

Civilón's story, had he not behaved with admirable savagery, reverting reassuringly to type once in the ring. The impressed crowd, and the equally impressed president of the plaza, granted Civilón a reprieve, so that although he underwent the punishments inflicted by the picador and the banderilleros, he was only caped, not killed, by the matador.

Bulls are, very occasionally, allowed to leave the ring alive if they have comported themselves with such casta that they recommended themselves for stud purposes. The fact that casta is meant to be inherited from the mother seems to be forgotten at this point in a desire to reward what is interpreted as courage on the animal's part.

Unfortunately, poor Civilón, saved from the sword, was still at the plaza, recovering from the wounds he received in the ring, when the Civil War broke out and troops entered Barcelona. Among the livestock slaughtered for food in the town was Civilón. As it happens, Lorca and the bull must have died within hours of each other.

My train heads further south as my ability to read fails me and a burning pain continues to shiver around my head and back. I take another pill, although I shouldn't do this without eating. Then again, if I eat, I know I'll be sick. I make do with drinking water and looking at the vaguely Middle Eastern mountains rearing up, the colour of sunset above their hard, slate shadow. Outside, there is strong, warm light now and a sky high with feathers of cloud. Inside, there are the nuns—all old, but remarkably unwrinkled. I wonder if holiness prevents creasing. There are two hours left of my journey and all I want to do is lie down. But instead I only shut my eyes and think of seeing—of the bull's way of seeing.

In my First-Year Physics class we had to dissect bull's (or more probably cow's) eyes in an effort to understand lenses. No one else was very keen on the task, so I found myself with a tiny queue of eyes, willingly donated by squeamish classmates, waiting for my knife. The eyes were, of course, beautiful. Once the choroid and sclerotic coats had been cut through and the translucent, vitreous and aqueous humours removed, the back of the retina was revealed: iridescent and magical. The knowledge that I was seeing something which was made for seeing, and which was itself secretly lovely, hypnotised me. Beyond the tedious and inaccurate drawings we all had to make, indicating the transected organ's form and function, this was a private delight—the kind of thing an old-time Jesuit would have held up as evidence of God's transcendent workmanship.

But the lesson of the bull's eye was misleading. Just as life is not as simple or comprehensible as my school led me to believe, just as the realities of sex have borne little relation to the blurred photograph of one locust balanced on another locust, which was the beginning and end of my formal sex education, so the use of a bovine eye to represent that of a human was less than helpful. Why? Because they are not the same. And, although the points of difference are of little interest to the general public, they are of central importance to the corrida and the matador on the toro's third bad day—the one that ends with the ring and the bull's virtually assured destruction.

First, if you ever get the chance, examine a cow's eye. It will be just as honey brown and benevolent as you'd expect, but look closer and you'll see that its pupil forms a long, thin, horizontal slit. The grain of the eye, the small drifts and flecks of colour, seem to disappear into this dark line, almost as if it were an opened flaw in a thick liquid. And, of course, the bovine eyes, *in situ*, are placed at the sides of the head.

Both these facts mean that, although a cow or a bull will turn its head inquisitively to face a movement, it doesn't actually see that movement in anything like the way we do. As far as research and observation can tell, any bovine, including the toro de lidia, will perceive anything more than roughly ten feet away rather poorly. The left and right fields of vision do not integrate, and so don't produce the kind of stereoscopic vision that humans or primates have. This leads many theorists to agree that toros have a large blind area or "anticone of [matador] immunity," directly to the front of their heads.

Research seems to show that animals without binocular vision are less stimulated by movements which run towards their temples. This makes a lot of sense. A toro, for example, pushing its head forwards, eyes largely passive, will see most of the world head towards it as a unified movement towards the back of its head—the things which stand out—like the flick of a cape—are the things which move out of this mass drift. This may actually begin to explain why toros charge at threats—running forwards tones down the visual input from the back-

ground and heightens their perception of the errant target. It would also explain why a man standing still,
unless he's directly in the bull's path, can be safe—he'll
simply fit in with the general, less stimulating, drift of
the landscape. And if you consider that movements
going towards the nose of the bull—against the usual
flow—are something immensely stimulating, it suddenly makes sense that the *pase natural*, a cape pass
which moves the cloth across the toro's leading eye in a
noseward direction, is regarded as the pass upon which
all toreo is founded and is the pass which always lures
the bull forward for the final sword thrust. In fact, most
passes move nosewards, across the leading eye. The
matador's experiential knowledge of how to play the
toro, the aficionado's rules and regulations for who
should stand where to get what result, are all based on
simple anatomy. Or, to put it another way, the acres of
poetic theorising and the yards of geometrical and technical theorising by observers of the corrida all come
down to the simplicity of two different species respond-
ing to each other as best they can, the simplicity of a
man trying to keep himself alive by thinking and feeling
beyond the speed of his own and the bull's reflexes.

The bull is also, of course, colour blind. So the red
rag to the bull doesn't have to be red—although the
magenta, yellow and red used in the toreros' capes all
have long wavelengths and are easy for the bull to see.

Naturally the presumed "blind spot," or "cone of
immunity," or "anticone of immunity" to the front of
the toro's head is also utilised by the matador—it certainly helps to make sense of the bull's inability to tell
the cape from the man and its desire to pursue the

movements of the cloth. For example, the flick of a cape from the blind area, into—say—the left field of vision will attract the bull and separate it from the matador who may be slightly visible in the right field, or even not visible at all. Equally, certain manoeuvres performed in front of the bull (without touching it) may not be as risky as they look, because the bull may be only very vaguely aware of them, while standing side-on to the bull, directly in one of its fields of vision, may look cowardly, but be decidedly dangerous.

A point to bear in mind would be that the bull, though not exactly an animal mastermind, does not go through life constantly amazed that the object heading noseward across its left field of vision so closely resembles the object which, soon after, heads earward across its right field of vision. The toro is used to the way it sees and has an instinctive feel for speed and direction, just as the torero does. This instinctive understanding of the bull's reactions helped keep matadors alive long before any scientific examinations of taurine visual systems. The toro, however well-explained, still remains dangerous and one mistake from the matador can still prove it.

Just before we reach Granada, chatter breaks out—it won't be long before we leave each other, so we can talk, some of us will be home soon and are glad. One of the nuns suddenly buttonholes a back-packer with an innocent grin and says "I am a Catholic"—in case we'd been wondering.

Off the train, the nuns turn girlish, scampering out of the station and folding themselves into a tiny car, driven by a rather raffish young priest. I drag my bag out past a huge poster showing Lorca's face and advertising cultural events of which he may or may not have approved—death having removed any real element of personal preference from his endorsements. Out at the taxi rank, I stand in soft, tepid air and watch bats circle the lamp-posts, on the hunt. I think of the first toros I ever saw, dying one after the other in edited corrida highlights on Spanish cable TV. I'd been flicking through the channels available in a London hotel and stopped, caught by the sight of successive animals standing, heads low, tongues protruding, while successive matadors advanced, a weird kind of weight in every slow step across the sand. Death was coming, startlingly obvious—the secret we rarely see—but the bulls just stood and panted, uncomprehending. I remember I took the symbolism to heart, considered our helplessness when it comes to the end, when we meet the pantomime surprise of death, the one we should always be expecting but never quite do.

I wonder again why Lorca came back to Granada, why he came home, why he took that last risk and came looking for extinction.

Chapter Four

Drop by Drop—The Making
of a Torero

"Write a story about a young man . . . who was brought up to fawn upon rank, to kiss priests' hands, and to worship others' thoughts, thankful for every morsel of bread, often whipped, going to his lessons without galoshes, who fought, tortured animals, and loved dining out with rich relations, playing the hypocrite before God and man through no necessity, but from a sheer awareness of his own insignificance—write how this young man squeezes the slave out of himself drop by drop and then wakes up one fine morning to discover that in his veins flows not the blood of a slave, but of a real human being . . ."*

Sorry to burden you with such a long quote. It's a translation from the Russian playwright and master of the short story A. P. Chekhov, and the usual academics have played the usual academic games about whether the piece is autobiographical or not. Why reproduce Anton Pavlovich here? Because, doctor that he was, he let himself die slowly of neglected TB?

*Anton Pavlovich Chekhov in a letter to A. S. Suvorin, 7 January 1889.

No. Even I'm not that obsessed with death.

Chekhov is here because, paraphrasing his own youth or not, he's summing up, as beautifully as we'd expect, the burn of self-perpetuating outrage that leads some individuals on to vocations, to larger-than-life lives, to fantasies fulfilled, transformative works and pyrotechnic extinctions: that leads them on to dreams and monuments.

Think of it for a moment—the sense of constricted potential that gnaws, deeper than ambition, that makes each small town smaller, each deprivation a constant weight, that can tip despair into desperation, into desperate acts. And then listen for the voice that tells you the daily humiliations of the world are absolutely all that you deserve. And then there's the *other* voice, the one that says you were made for better things, *are* better than these things, that you can escape them by excelling, by finding that certain something that seems to be calling you. It seems a sweet deal—accept your vocation and save your identity, or, should you happen to have one, your soul. And, if the two voices don't tear you apart, then maybe, with a little help from chance, you really will do it. Perhaps, having been invisible for all of this long, hard while, you will make yourself as much yourself as you know you need to be.

I'm not saying this is the beginning of every rags-to-riches story, every tale of the plucky kid snatched from obscurity by the gift of a magical voice, left hook, healing touch, eye for colour, feel for the instrument, knack for construction, way with words, way with bulls—fill in the blank as you'd like. I'm only suggesting this may not be far from the truth in a number of cases. So, when speaking of toreros, this is where I start.

Not all toreros, of course, are born in anything like the gutter. But many of history's finest have been peasants, slum-dwellers, young men who grew up hungry, all too aware of how little they had to lose. This said, on the journey to the ring, perspectives change. In the face of the corrida, and the toros, a simple continuation of existence can seem all that anybody could desire. But away from taurine duties, more beguiling changes lie in wait. Top matadors have long seen their skills remake their lives. As their reputation rises, new circles of acquaintance flower: suddenly they know film stars, millionaires, European royalty. Journalists and authors track them from hotel to hotel.

Having struggled for bread and fought in a borrowed *traje de luces** one year, the next they'll be buying property, retaining employees. They'll discover that celebrity can make almost anything possible: the more numbing types of sexual excess, or drink and drugs enough to still even a practising matador's nerves, or ludicrous and sometimes strangely fugitive wealth. Perhaps they'll even find love, a growing family with real security—except for that fear when the man of the house goes out to work, that ache in the air on corrida afternoons.

Even now, when standards of living are generally at least comfortable in Spain, country boys and middle-class city sons still find toreo propelling them into an alien territory: the life of a rock star, a latter-day prince.

*"Suit of lights"—the traditional garb of the torero in the ring.

They get what they want or, one might even say, what seems to have wanted them. And sometimes it feeds them and sometimes it eats them alive.

Historically, matadors might come to their deaths in a number of more or less traditional ways. They might die of TB—raised on a poor diet and kept unhealthy by an occupation which—now, as then—relies surprisingly little on strength, but which either starves toreros of fights and income, or demands they rattle through a seemingly endless tour of plaza after plaza. Blurring through hotel rooms and sleeping on the road, eating on the run, matadors could face bulls three, four or more times a week, trying to work around still-healing injuries through a season that lasted, and still lasts, in Spain from April to October and which might then continue in Mexico for the winter. For those who kept healthy, despite repeated exposure to sheer exhaustion, gorings in the ring still lay in wait and could easily lead to wounds that turned gangrenous. The day's plaza might not even have its own infirmary—simple blood loss could take a torero before he ever reached an operating table. And, for those with a taste for physical recreations away from the rigours of the corrida, there was always the slow way to decay offered by syphilis.

Antibiotics and advances in medical facilities and techniques have made the modern torero's life safer, but the rigours of the *temporada*, the season for corridas, are now even greater with more and more toreros going straight to Peru, Mexico, Ecuador, Chile, when the European season is over and then heading back for plazas in Spain and the South of France, pretty much as soon as it opens again. The stresses of the life, the wearing proximity of death, the shock of injury, can produce a prodigious appetite for alcohol and drugs, a tendency towards depression, or a commitment to risk that can bring suicide a touch too close, in and out of the ring. All this the reward for men who have won their boyhood dream, who have managed to become full matadors. Be careful, as they say, of what you pray for—you might get it.

Which is something to consider as I stand in the Huerta de San Vicente in Granada. This was the summer house of the Lorca family: thick white walls, shining placidly in the sun, beneath a painfully bright sky. The place used to be surrounded by fields, I'm told: now it's marooned in a modern park, dedicated to Lorca, set hard on the outskirts of the city. Only the Huerta's small garden, the blossoms that trail over its porch, the languidly tall windows, the slim balconies, give any sense of a slower, more genteel, rural past.

I enter through the doorway where Lorca was photographed smiling, avuncular in proletarian overalls, with him a vaguely bashful little boy and a slightly older girl who hangs on his arm. Inside, the rooms are cool, simple: in the hall, I see the sofa where he was pictured once laughing, head tilted back, eyes wide. The sensation that I must have been here before is unmistakable, as is the certain knowledge that someone is missing, somehow still expected to come home.

The young guide talks us through the last few days of Lorca's life with an affectionate sadness. A different variety of regret, transformed by anger, commerce, guilt, has left Granada full of Lorca posters, Lorca postcards, Lorca T-shirts, Lorca sculptures and Lorca books.

Hardly a shop window is without his face. And he wasn't exactly an unknown author when he came here for that last time in the summer of '36. It seems remarkable that the fame which made him such a tempting victim couldn't also have kept him safe. His death was a propaganda disaster for the Nationalists—but every expression of public outrage was far too late to save him.

I go upstairs, see the poet's room, his desk, the comfortable arrangement of a space intended to fit around a writer. For some reason, I reach for the light switch as I walk out again—not to turn on the light, only to touch the switch, as he must have touched it. The guide watches—he must have seen this kind of thing before.

In the next room are some Lorca manuscripts, laid out in cases: first editions of this and that, hardly the most gripping display I've ever seen. But, still, I have to wait with my face turned away until the rest of the party has gone, because I am crying. I'm in the house of a man who was called to write, who did the human joyful thing which is to put words onto paper. He made himself a writer, a famous man, a target. He was hurt by his love, betrayed by his vocation—something else that shouldn't happen, another sin to add to murder, but a complicated one—a sin without a sinner.

Back in the peace of the garden, blinking in the sun as it sharpens towards noon, I know this is where Lorca stayed until he went into hiding in the Calle de Angulo. This is the garden where he saw his caretaker, Gabriel Perea, tied to a tree and whipped by Nationalist thugs. When Lorca intervened he was knocked to the ground and kicked. And then he was recognised—Federico García Lorca, friend of the Republican Government, left-wing writer and queer. The Huerta de San Vicente is the last Lorca saw of the life he'd made before he went into hiding. In one of the neat, low hedges a party of scrawny kittens is practising lopsided pounces, padding and tumbling through practice kills, raising the dust.

I had meant to ask someone here if they could tell me where 1 Calle de Angulo is—it's not marked on my map. I had meant to lay claim to the courtesy a visiting writer might expect here now. But I only feel sickened with myself. I didn't defend my vocation, couldn't handle the smallest, lowest grade of threat. So how can I say I'm a writer in this of all places.

And I don't want to go to the Calle de Angulo, even if it still exists. I don't want to know where it is. I want his memorial in my mind to be the Huerta—a place where he was mainly happy.

I walk back into town slowly—slowly being the way I now always walk—and I make my way up to the Alhambra, Granada's Moorish pleasure ground. With its topiary and pools, its tilework and filigreed stone, I can see that the place is lovely, but the pain across my shoulders and under my head seems to make everything distant, it blurs the heat. And Lorca is here, too, intervening—the echo of a reproach—the ghost posing in snapshots with friends by the old walls, beside one of the pools, grinning, secure.

Feeling light-headed, I try to eat in one of the small restaurants on the Alhambra's hill. I'm already in a foul mood and being surrounded by the bourgeoisie of Granada doesn't help, although it's hardly their fault that they're still alive, chatting, playing with their children, calling to acquaintances. I order *rabo de toro—*

bull's tail—which may or may not come from a toro de lidia. Granada does have a bull ring and the meat from all toros does end up in butcher's shops, the possibility is there. In Britain, this dish would be illegal, of course—it's beef still shamelessly on the bone—but the transgression is hardly thrilling.

A deep ceramic dish arrives, filled with oxtails, vegetables and gravy and I know it's absurd to be eating something stewed when the temperature's in the eighties, but I'm having a personal cold spell, shivering. The sections of tail taste much like any other kind of beef, are tender and slightly gelatinous, fiddly to deconstruct. Stripped of their flesh, the tail fragments are delicate with, here and there, a tiny joint—I stare at them and think of finger bones.

And I look at my own hands and remember again that I nearly said, that I nearly did say I was a writer, that I nearly did say that out loud, but then couldn't open my mouth because I was ashamed—an apostate in the house of a martyr. I let my blood thin out a long time ago, drop by drop, back to nothing again. And now I'm hot, sweating hot, suddenly and the pills are making me think of eating my own fingers and I may well throw up if I don't change my subject, change my mind.

So I'll think about the story of Juan Belmonte, matador. This is an old story, but the progression it charts would not be too unfamiliar today—vocation, its thefts and its gifts, they stay the same.

Belmonte was born on 14th April 1892 in a slum quarter of Seville. He was the family's first child and might, therefore, have been expected to grow up and help his struggling parents support themselves and their ten subsequent children. In reality, he fell in love with the corrida, his earliest memory recalling the cries announcing "El Espartero's" death in the ring. He became a boy who would practise fledgling cape passes on anything that moved—bicycles, carriages, dogs—a troubling youngster, flirting with delinquency, and of little assistance to his small-time shopkeeper relatives. Belmonte's teenage years were overshadowed by spasms of filial shame and "an inexhaustible energy [which] drove me on without telling me where I was going."* His need, his vocation, moved in him beyond his understanding, beyond his will to resist, but it had a generosity he could touch when he found that, "with a cape in my hands, I, who was such a small and insignificant person with a vast inferiority complex, felt myself so much superior to the other boys who were physically stronger than I."

After bruising afternoons spent facing an inn's resident toro, after dangerous, thrilling nights spent in ganadería fields learning to handle a cape when it counts, learning the physical language of the bulls, a deep sympathy for the reactions and instincts of another species, Belmonte began to understand his own nature. His belief in his own identity as a matador was woundingly intense, as was his frustration with a corrida "so hide-bound, so rigidly and exhaustively hemmed in by canons of immemorial antiquity" that he despaired of ever realising his true self.

*This, and the quotations on pages 66, 67 and 70–71, are from *Killer of Bulls*, Juan Belmonte's autobiography.

Belmonte tried his hand at anarchic rural capeas where half-starved young would-be matadors tried to do their best with over-experienced or simply impossible bulls, or the faster, more dangerous cows. He even once presented himself, along with his band of rowdy, aficionado companions, at a tienta. His reception from the lordly, land-owning ganadero was predictably contemptuous. Finally, "Calderón," a professional banderillero and a friend of Belmonte's father, took young Juan under his wing, helped him to a trial on a ganadería and spread Belmonte's legend as a great matador before his early efforts as an apprentice in low-grade plazas gave the slightest clue that greatness was beckoning.

I have a photograph of Belmonte at about this time— not yet a full professional, but a rising light, he stands, carefully giving the camera the kind of gently relentless stare he must already have levelled at dozens of bulls. His attitude makes him every inch the matador, but his body lets him down. Emerging from an impossibly solid-looking overcoat, his head and hands are tiny. And, under a cheap haircut, there is the flat forehead, the huge, skewed nose, the trademark, prognathous, Popeye jaw. Here, as he would all his life, he looks like a savage caricature of himself, like a punchy boxer, a village idiot—except for the eyes. Even in long-dead, stilted black and white and caught at the very start of his career, Belmonte has an extraordinary focus, a quietly deadly poise.

And he needed it. Like all novilleros—formally apprenticed matadors—Belmonte faced the toros that full matadors rejected: the usual squint-horned, walleyed collection of bulls too wily, too barmy, too nasty, too big and too unpredictable for anyone sane to be willing to face them. But Belmonte did face them, sometimes hampered by only partially closed wounds from previous encounters, and he didn't die. He suffered terrible failures and humiliations—bulls he couldn't kill, bulls he screamed at to kill him. He saw his energies sapped by an impossible love affair and mindless manual labour. But, just when his strength and hopes were flagging, when it seemed his vocation might actually leave him be and let him settle for his smaller self, he entered the ring in Valencia and had a good day. He ended it in the hospital, but with his reputation more than intact, and with a taste for the skills, for the new life already growing for him in the ring, and for the love of the crowd.

Next, in Seville, he remembers, "I simply fought as I believed one ought to fight, without a thought outside my own faith in what I was doing. With the last bull, I succeeded for the first time in my life in delivering myself body and soul to the pure joy of fighting without being consciously aware of an audience. When I was playing the bulls alone in the country I used to talk to them; and that afternoon I held a long conversation with the bull . . ." He was gored in the leg as he went in for the kill—as he repeatedly dreamed he would be gored—but he was carried out of the Prince's Gate of the La Maestranza plaza in triumph: Seville's ultimate accolade.

Because anyone watching him could see he had something new, something to bring on duende. Just as, decades later, Monty Roberts would learn the language of wild horses by observing them on the prairie, Belmonte had learned his bulls in the ganaderías on the Tablada beyond Seville. This deeply assimilated knowledge joined with Belmonte's certainty that he was a frail man, unable to run and with limited stamina. These two influences—along with the drive still gripping him in its wonderful, terrible teeth—meant that Belmonte rapidly developed an entirely new and apparently suicidal approach to toreo.

Belmonte brought the bull closer to his body than ever before, stood still more than ever before, moved the emphasis away from the kill and onto the cape work preceding it, the strange, brief period during which a man and a wild animal can appear to co-operate. He began to explore the secrets of the flicking cloth. Aficionados were, as usual, either enraged or entranced by this alteration to the status quo. Many agreed with "Gueritta"—Rafael Guerra Bejerano, then a retired matador—who is frequently quoted as saying, "Hurry up and see him fight, because if you don't see him soon you'll never see him." Much the same is said now of the young phenomenon "El Juli." In the corrida, excellence and tragedy go hand in hand.

So Belmonte, like many before and since, began to learn the lessons of fame. He now had the money to bail his younger brothers out of the orphanage and support his family, but he also had to deal with regiments of worthy causes and would-be adherents. He couldn't walk out in the street, or go into a bar, without being recognised, propositioned, importuned, mobbed.

Fortunately, Belmonte didn't begin his career—as many do—by being too deeply in debt to his *apoderado*, or manager. Taking part in a corrida involves the hire of a cuadrilla—usually including picadors and their horses—transportation, the hire or purchase of the fabulously expensive traje de luces for the matador—if not the rest of the cuadrilla—the usual, institutionalised backhanders to journalists, outlay for advertising and numberless other extras. A young man who wants to be a torero has to have a wealthy and—preferably—influentially taurine family, or must convince someone to invest in his future and to arrange corridas for him, in the hope that he will prove himself and all will have a share of potentially grotesque profits at a later date.

A young woman, or a non-Spanish aspirant, will find acquiring an apoderado and an entrée to the corrida even more difficult. John Fulton, the American matador, never felt fully accepted by the taurine establishment, despite some greatly acclaimed performances. Christina Sánchez, well-placed in last year's professional rankings, retired from the corrida this year, after a bad South American season.* She very publicly condemned the macho plaza regime which meant she could never gain the engagements, the income or the respect of a similarly ranked torero.

And the old-fashioned option of leaping into the bull ring during a corrida as an *espontáneo* and trying to show off a few cape passes before you're dragged away to jail is no longer viable. The professional union bars any espontáneo from taking part in a corrida for a year after

*Torero retirals are, of course, notoriously reversible. There are also rumours that Sánchez's reasons for withdrawal from the ring may be more pressingly maternal than professional. Phlegmatic aficionados note that Sánchez has been discriminated against all her career and wonder why she has suddenly chosen this year to withdraw in protest.

their leap. Spontaneous amateurs do, after all, put not only themselves at risk, but also the professional torero who is trying to play the bull and who wants nothing less than an inexperienced opportunist spooking it, or inadvertently teaching it how to identify the cape with the man on the ground.

The travails of entering the profession and the reliance on the apoderado and his finances can mean that even successful matadors find themselves mortgaged to their apoderado. This also adds a commercial pressure to the obvious personal ones which lead to the breeding of more docile bulls, to matadors' refusals to fight "bulls of death" like the Miuras, and to a range of bull-pacifying and matador-saving skulduggery we'll discuss later.

Belmonte fought his way into the aristocratic and highly conservative world of the corrida against the odds and took his *alternativa* in Madrid on 16th October 1913—the same year an espontáneo was gored to death in the ring at Calatayud. The alternativa is a matador's graduation ceremony. It requires that the novillero appears on the bill with full professional matadors at the Las Ventas ring in the capital and then, with bowed heads, an embrace and the passing over of the cape and killing sword, one of the professionals gives the aspirant the honour of causing the bull's death. In Belmonte's case, an older torero, "Machaquito," acted as this kind of godfather. "Machaquito" played a bull and then handed over the kill to Belmonte, alternating with him—hence, alternativa. Alternativas taken elsewhere in Spain or overseas must be confirmed again in Madrid.

Belmonte was now truly a matador, a killer of bulls, working in first-class plazas and killing four- to six-year-old bulls, as opposed to the three- to four-year-olds that a novillero faces. His professional debut heralded what is generally known as the Golden Age, during which Belmonte redefined toreo and was joined in a personally cordial, but immensely intense, rivalry with another master matador—"Joselito," José Gómez, who had taken his alternativa the year before. Between 1913 and 1920, rival fans rallied to their respective favourite, aficionados found a new enthusiasm for the plaza and the stakes seemed to rise with each corrida. Belmonte and Joselito needed each other, gave each other a new will to excel.

And they also learned together that public adoration could turn to vociferous, even violent, contempt if they couldn't be great enough heroes, if they couldn't live up to the public's impossible hopes, the expectation that transcendent moments would be scattered out like pennies from every encounter in the ring. The drive towards more and more exciting, and therefore dangerous, toreo spread beyond the two rivals, who had their own share of wounds and narrow escapes. Casualties among toreros in all the plazas went up. The public were loving their matadors to death.

Despite the predictions of doom, Belmonte continued playing bulls and breaking the rules. The sacred theory of "territories" or "terrains," formulated by aficionados to codify the proper areas to be occupied by man or bull at x or y moment, were not for Belmonte. "The bull has no territory, because it is not a reasoning creature and there are no surveyors to lay down its boundaries."

And then, in 1920, it happened. The day after appearing in a corrida with Belmonte, "Joselito" went out into the plaza at Talavera de la Reina. The preceding afternoon he'd been booed by the crowd and had a cushion thrown at his head, hardly fit treatment for a man risking his life. It's said that someone in the crowd shouted to "Joselito" that he hoped the matador would be killed in his next corrida. The remark, real or imagined, has passed into legend, because "Joselito" *was* killed in that next Talavera corrida by a bull called "Bailador."

"Bailador" was, so the story goes, a long-sighted animal. When "Joselito" backed away from it before the kill to adjust his *muleta,** he simultaneously divided his focus of attention and moved into the bull's best area of vision. This is the reality behind the theory of forbidden and permissible territories—"Joselito" inadvertently placed himself in a life-threatening position. "Bailador" rushed in and caught his man unawares, goring "Joselito's" left leg and lifting him up. As he was lifted, "Joselito" fell onto the other horn and it buried its full length in his stomach. He was dead before they could carry him out of the ring.

Belmonte felt the loss deeply—whatever antipathy their fans enjoyed generating, the two matadors were as close as one might expect men to be, having faced death together so many times. Belmonte continued the round

---

*The small red cape, stiffened with a rod, which is used by the matador during the final passes which lead to the kill. Only the matador can use the muleta.

of hotels and plazas, adoration and ridicule, more lonely than before, his dream profession becoming a kind of mobile imprisonment. There were times when he couldn't face it, when he could only lie and stare at the ceiling. He fell into a pattern of intermittent depression and grew to hate the multiplicity of forces—emotional, physical and financial—which could separate him from that first deep, luminous connection with the vocation which had chosen him. The thing which had made him happier than he could ever have imagined, the thing which lit his soul, had also condemned him. Like many matadors, Belmonte retired several times but, having been given a way to fulfil his greatest passion, he came to understand how powerless he was to live without it. Be careful what you pray for, you might love it.

After his last retiral in 1935, the Civil War saw Belmonte appearing occasionally in the plaza as a *rejoneador*—a torero who plays and spears the bull from horseback. But the wartime shortage of bulls and then his increasing age meant that his days as a matador were effectively over by the time peace broke out. He could breed toros de lidia, he could watch from the president's box at the Seville plaza, he could endure or enjoy the attention his instantly recognisable face always brought, but the heart of the corrida was closed to him.

On Sunday, 8th April 1962, Belmonte came home from church and surprised hands at his ganadería by going out on horseback for a session of acoso y derribo. Then he played several toros with the cape, despite onlookers' concerns for his health—he was, after all, a frail man a few days from his seventieth birthday. He then demanded that another, massive seed bull should be brought for him to play and, when tactful excuses were made to explain its absence, he went back to the ranch house, had a drink and wrote a short note. And then he shot himself.

I leave Granada by the night train. I want to reverse that last sleeping-car journey Lorca made to come home. Although this is stupid and pointless, I want to leave on his behalf. But, for some reason, I find that I'm already late when I get out of the hotel and then I can't find a cab. My progress takes on the cloying quality of an anxiety dream. Even when I do flag down a taxi, we are stopped by every light, delayed and delayed until I begin to wonder if I really will be able to get away.

But, of course, in the end I make it, find my carriage, drag my bag inside. Then, locked in my little cell for the night, I dowse my face at the minute metal sink, pull down the top bunk, turn off the light and clamber up to lie.

I only begin to relax when the engine starts to haul, when the rhythm of lights at the window has settled itself to a scattering, easy rush. The pain isn't good tonight, it's scaring me again: I've taken too many pills and I know I won't sleep, but I can watch the night as it passes. I am alive and making a journey that never was, unravelling a mistake, sleeper by sleeper, back to Atocha Station, Madrid.

Chapter Five

Acts of Faith

I'm in the Plaza Mayor, Madrid, and feeling uneasy, prone to vertigo—too little sleep and too much history. During the Spanish Inquisition, prisoners from all over Spain were brought here to discover what more or less appalling future waited for them. Corridas were held here until 1847 and, in something over three hundred years, the plaza has seen executions, the inaugurations of four saints and, of course, the burning of numberless heretics. Currently the place looks only calm and sternly elegant—the kind of thing we don't do well in Britain—a quiet, European square with vaulted stone arcades around its margins, an equestrian statue at its heart, a judicious scatter of cafés with alfresco tables and prices implying a cover charge for the view.

This afternoon, I'm almost the only one sitting outside—it is, after all, pissing down with rain. But, while water drips off the nearest, sodden parasol and onto my back, I am attempting to eat lunch. I thought a spot of fresh air and food would do me good and I find that I'm now unwilling, or just unable, to change my mind. I am, in any case, experiencing problems of belief—this particular piece of reality seems unconvincing. I have no faith in it. Now and then, the damp breeze splashes a fraction of the downpour across my plate, but I can't say that I care: wet or dry, I don't seem to be able to taste the food. I had a bad night on the train back from Granada—stayed unpleasantly awake for the duration.

Out of politeness, the waiter talks to me in bad English and, for similar reasons, I talk back in bad Spanish and the plaza kicks and ripples when I look at it because I am too tired to see. I have a few taurine magazines with me, newly bought, and am grinding away at one particular text—a piece on toreros' suicidal exhibitionism. But reading proves tricky, the print swimming back and forth in unhelpful whorls and adding to the generally liquid atmosphere. Still, even the unco-operative print is better than the naked heat of the photographs, the blare of each magenta and yellow *capote de brega*,* the lurid colours of the trajes de luces, the bright cloaking of blood on each bull's shoulders, the *banderillas*,† caught in the midst of movement and dust, fanning out from the morrillo like an absurd crest, the weird prefiguring of an impact yet to come. Anything beyond the monochrome hurts my eyes.

---

*The large cape the matador uses for his first passes with the bull.
†The 27-inch dowel-stemmed dart, metal-tipped with a single barb, three pairs of which are intended to be thrown into the area around the bull's morrillo during the second phase of the corrida. The wooden stems are decorated with coloured paper strips. Banderillas, once placed, used to stand fairly proud in the bull's flesh, but have lately been made with a collapsible neck which makes them less of an obstruction to the matador as they now flop and rattle like surreal dreadlocks against the bull's haunches.

But, in the inside pocket of my coat, I have tickets for the corrida. I paid for them this morning, asked for a good seat and may, for all I know, have got one. So on Sunday there'll be no more photos unless I take them: on Sunday I'll see the corrida, the real thing.

And already I'm participating in something that many Britons find morally repugnant, something to do with donkey-torturing Spaniards, a primitive and—thankfully—thoroughly foreign ritual. Either that, or I've just given money to the corrida, the darling of the Politically Incorrect—of people who might find it amusing to read about bare-knuckle fighting, or even go to watch, who praise the hunt, cigar-smoking, the more picturesque types of drug abuse, people who enjoy a good joke about the Holocaust, because that doesn't mean they're being bigoted, ignorant or simply inhuman, it means they've decided to be Post-Modernist. These are also people who may tell you that cruelty is more real than tenderness, but who still always seem to want tenderness for themselves—less real, or not. These are people for whom I have very little respect.

The RSPCA (and I do respect them) would tell me that, by paying the price of my ticket, I've just helped to support a barbaric sport and that, without tourist pounds and dollars, the corrida would collapse for lack of funds. This isn't actually true. Although many Spaniards, and particularly Catalans, have little or no affection for the corrida, and although there is a core of staunch Spanish opponents to its every manifestation, it is currently enjoying a massive rise in popularity at home and in the wider, Spanish-speaking world. The corrida is now a multi-million-dollar, international industry, very well supported by television companies anxious to buy broadcast rights, and more than capable of replacing other "bloodless" Southern French and Portuguese styles of bull spectacle. Which makes my financial input factually unimportant, but I don't deny that it still has a moral significance. So, before I outline the final preparations of man and bull for their meeting in the ring, I will explain my position vis-à-vis the humans and the animals in the plaza.

I believe that human beings are animals. By this, I mean that humanity does not prosper and, indeed, endangers its long-term survival by forgetting that it is reliant upon, and connected to, the animal world. Our fundamentals are "animal"—we eat, we defecate, we procreate, we die—we are moving meat.

I do not mean by this that we can excuse our excesses of inhumanity by tracing their roots back to "animal" behaviour. The anthropological theories of—to pick a notorious example—Prof. Raymond Dart portrayed South African early hominids attacking each other like Siamese fighting fish on speed and, thereby, handily easing our species' culpability in every act of human violence conducted since, from unsightly jostling in the Post Office queue, to Torquemada the Grand Inquisitor's tortures, to the Korean War and on and—of course—on.

But Dart's theories were not based on a close examination of available evidence. The remains Dart found at Taung showed clear signs of animal, not human, attack, but the good professor was already convinced of man's essentially aggressive nature and was also pleasantly aware, in a curiously child-like way, that his spin on our historical self-portrait was just plain *exciting*.

Man as animalistic killer makes a good story. Head-lines announcing that early human beings were brain-sucking, viciously cannibal monsters always go down well. Unlike those which suggest that art, co-operation, language and culture are our inheritance and our responsibility. And the fact that these four civilised virtues were present far earlier in our history than sophisticated Western humanity would like to think and in far more foreign places than we'd like to find them can prove discomfiting. It also makes stealing—or hav-ing stolen—land and resources in countries already inhabited by "primitive" people far less palatable and, legally, far more troublesome. So Dart, Konrad Lorenz, Robert Ardrey and their ilk have prospered by pander-ing to our worst, or least demanding, expectations of ourselves and—perhaps inadvertently—have given an impressive array of "truths" to those who would manip-ulate us towards anything from a callously commercial mindset to genocide.

Science, for me, proves that we are animals who are meant for better things, who are better than these things—this tangible mish-mash of hormones and habits, instincts and mortality. On my good days, faith would have proved that, too.

So, naturally, I also have a problem with human beings who think that other human beings who happen to be Gypsies, Jews, Spaniards, single mothers, Serbs, Moslems, Albanians, matadors, are in some way less human than they are. Equally, I know that human beings can be made less human. I know that humanity's images of its own nature are often a self-fulfilling prophecy, that even our own, smaller, private ideas of ourselves can excuse torture and murder. Or they can make a life of saintly sacrifice seem beautifully unavoidable. Our actions and our intentions feed upon each other, letting the real and the imagined self echo, repeat and amplify both nightmares and blessed revelations. In word, in thought, in deed we define and create ourselves. And our relationship with ourselves is reflected in our treatment of others, in our attitude towards other lives, including the lives of animals.

Cruelty to animals has long been regarded as a precursor of psychopathic behaviour. In fact, certain types of animal abuse (primarily, where the animal is dominated, tortured and killed as a "practice human") are taken in America to be such a clear indication of future violence to humans that they can result, on conviction, in highly punitive custodial sentences. I have a great deal of sympathy with this view.

I also know the recently identified blood chemistry which may lead psychopaths to crave the emotional intensity of risk-taking has also been found in many matadors. But I do not believe that matadors are psychopaths—they are simply among those human beings who crave the emotional intensity which is a part of taking risks. As I have outlined, in my opinion, matadors' actions in the plaza have a great deal to do with both a personal and a wider kind of faith, an intermingling of fear, superstition, Catholic iconography and both Christian and pre-Christian urges to understand the termination of life and to celebrate survival.

This, for me, means that the corrida is not a sport, although it is treated on Spanish TV much as any sport would be, and—despite being reported in the "Culture" sections of Spanish newspapers—is developing the trappings of other modern sporting events. Some rings now have giant screens for action replays or even—blasphemous rumour, this—sponsorship logos on the toreros' trajes. The corrida is also not an art, although it has been described as such by its admirers, most notably by a group of artists who wished to describe Juan Belmonte as an artist and, by extension, to define toreo as art. The corrida can sometimes create the effect of art (as can, for that matter, a voodoo ceremony, a funeral, or a high mass) but it is divided against itself, because of the unpredictability of the bull, because of the numerous abuses of its own laws, because it hopes to weaken the bull, but leave it glorious, to defend the matador, but give him something to overcome. The corrida, although it has its own rigours and remarkable individual toreros, currently lacks the overarching discipline, creative economy and communicative breadth of an art. It could also be said that its levels of cruelty and violence prevent it from being an art, that an art cannot exceed certain parameters of damage, that it cannot cause death.

I feel that the corrida is still very close to its origins in religion, that it is a religious ritual in a state of slow transition. The direction of this transition is generally away from the kill and towards the preparation for the kill, the cape passes where the man and bull can seem to reach an unlikely communion. I am, perhaps, not alone in this view of the corrida—in Politically Correct California, "bloodless" but none the less stressful corridas are permitted, but only as one part of a religious festival. The Politically Correct always have to allow others freedom of religious expression.

My opinion of the corrida does not mean that I excuse the ugliness which is undoubtedly an element in its composition. Historical or religious precedent does not make something right. Scots, for example, have historically been enthusiastic slave traders, witch burners and exploiters of child labour, but that doesn't mean I'm going to argue that all true Scots should love these activities, or that Scots should be allowed to perpetuate them as an expression of their culture. By the same token, as you might guess, I'm not exactly the fox-hunting, blood-sporting type. I dislike it when a custom which is very much to do with demonstrating historical class and privilege is dressed up as "part of nature." When genuinely a part of nature, animals and human beings hunt food they can eat only for as long as the hunt makes sense in terms of energy lost in pursuit, balanced against energy gained in consuming the prey. The British hunt is a ritual designed to reinforce a particular order of society and heaven help the farmer who doesn't want the hounds on his land or who feels aggrieved on learning that, in Merry Olde England, foxes were once imported from Europe by lovers of the chase and then released to restock British farmland stripped of foxes by over-enthusiastic hunts. Never mind keeping down vermin— the gentlemen must have their fun.

The corrida, as I've mentioned, also has its land-owning, aristocratic side which has never endeared it to the Left. But the lowly origins of the matadors and other toreros give them the populist appeal that—say—boxers might have in Britain. The poor can earn their way to glory with blood. The very role of the toreros (who are still called *peones*, or peasants) developed from that of the lowly, horseless assistants to the mounted gentlemen—*rejoneadors*—who fought the bulls with spears in the early Moorish and then Christian precursors of the corrida. The modern pre-eminence of the matador—an unmounted man who is still master of the peones—is, at this level, the triumph of the underdog.

But beyond questions of class and audience, there is the matter of life and death. The killing of the bulls and the genuine risk to the humans involved in their execution set the corrida in its own, unique classification: part entertainment, part outrage, part sacrament. Observers have seen it in elements of sport, blood sport, dance and theatre. Perhaps a more useful point of reference would be the *auto-da-fé*.*

You will remember that the auto-da-fé was the ritual public procession made by symbolically costumed sinners and heretics during the time of the Inquisition. It was a grimly ornate ceremony designed to both parade and punish the guilty. Their act of faith involved being given up by the Holy Inquisition (which could torture them, but not kill them) and then passed on to secular authorities empowered to continue their humiliation and torture and, in the most serious cases, to burn them at the stake. Each prisoner was dressed in a high pasteboard cap and a yellow tunic—the *sanbenito*—sometimes painted with the image of their coming punishment, including the flames of the funeral pyre. These yellow

*Portuguese: literally, "act of faith."

tunics were then hung in churches, bearing the wearer's name and verdict as trophies of the Inquisition. This spectacle was intended to be both terrible and sanctified—the ultimate fiesta.

And there do seem to be links between Spain's two troubling fiestas—the auto-da-fé and the corrida: the Christian and the Pagan ceremonies reflect and influence each other. The Moorish invasion of Spain in 711 had brought an artistic and organising influence to bear on the proto-corrida. The Christian Reconquista set it firmly under the disapproving control of the church of Rome as a popular, but suspect, reminder of other things un-Christian. In the fifteenth century the Inquisition emerged—a powerful political entity, separate from Rome's authority—and the auto-da-fé emerged as a new public phenomenon. For a period, the two fiestas developed side by side—both with dazzling costumes, a weight of ritual, the presence of death, the possibilities of redemption, a long walk to the plaza and another life, in this world or the next.

As the Inquisition, with its demand for symbols of Christian pain and sacrifice, waned in the seventeenth and eighteenth centuries, the corrida flourished, ever stronger, with its symbols borrowed from Pagan pain and sacrifice. To the corrida, the spilling of blood was, and largely remains, essential. For the Holy Inquisition, heretics were burned in the auto-da-fé because the church was—in theory, at least—forbidden to spill a drop of human blood. In the auto-da-fé, faith in God, the King and the church's power were publicly proved in acts of ultimate violence and their observation. In the corrida, the audience, even now, bears witness to a charged encounter between the human and the animal, to something beyond the level of articulated religion, to proof that a man can overcome the threat, even the actuality, of injury, for his own and perhaps his audience's sake.

This makes for a potentially anarchic, atheistic ritual. Yet, in a powerfully Catholic country, the corrida has also come to be a kind of modern Trial by Ordeal. It can display a single human being's frailty before God and the world, along with his faith in a sustaining power, a faith that rocks the watching crowd, pausing its breath, a faith that can bring someone back from the plaza alive. During the Civil War, both readings of the corrida were present. Nationalist corridas celebrated the church and might of the Right. Republican corridas celebrated the triumph of the common man.

But this still only explains a little of the corrida, not why I would choose to join its audience. So why am I in Madrid, why am I sitting in a plaza that quietly recalls both corridas and autos-da-fé, why did I come?

Because I was asked to?—that's no reason.

Because, once here, I can observe on your behalf?—that's part of the writer's duties, but I'm not exactly here as a writer and, in matters of morality, duty is no excuse.

Because I want to test what may be left of my abilities?—nearer.

Because I have nothing else to do?—nearer.

Because I am afraid to be idle with myself and alone?—yes.

Because this is something to occupy my mind?—yes.

Because I can be a witness to anything now?—yes.

I have, after all, seen animal sacrifice before. I've watched young goats stretched taut by the hooves, before and behind, and held for a still moment, bewildered into silence. And then I've seen their heads struck off in one long blur of metallic light, the blood coming after in ribbons, a hot flutter from their suddenly incomprehensible necks.

But that was quick, that was painless, that was unmistakably religious—a practical matter of feeding a temple's adherents, an impractical matter of faith. Nothing about that disturbed me—my predisposition has always been, after all, to pay the best of my attention, to try to know, to understand.

Which is why I'm here, really why I'm here—because I pay too much attention. I didn't sleep on the train because I spent last night remembering that I pay too much attention, remembering what I know and do not understand.

And this is the way I spend at least a part of every night. Because of that one night: the creaking in the hotel corridor and the heavy, small-hours air and the way he kissed me on both cheeks and said it would be all right because he'd be no good, that he would go and have sex with a woman that we neither of us knew, but it would be all right, because he'd be no good and he was sorry, although he didn't say for what.

Having paid my best attention, I remember this. This, and the time, just a little later, when I stood and felt nothing at all, thought nothing at all, and then the next, much longer period I spent beside the door, the bedroom door, listening to them, to him. Because I knew that I would never believe what was happening unless I had absolute proof and because I have this pre-disposition to pay the best of my attention, to try to know, to understand.

All I found out was that some things have no words for them, so why bother with words.

In the sleeping car, in my own bed, in all of the other hotel beds, this is what thoughts of the bulls can keep me from. This is the stupid little place where I left my faith. And I'm not in Madrid to get it back, only to see what I have to and then tell what I saw to you. Because I can see anything now and this is not a weakness but a strength. I'm here to understand something which is, by its nature, incomprehensible as a flutter of sudden blood. But that's all right, now I'm quite used to incom-prehensibility.

And if my portrait is in my words and thoughts and deeds then this isn't too impressive a picture. I do under-stand that. I have only poor reasons for being here. And there you have it—my preparation for the plaza.

But, because this is why you're here and reading, I'll set down other preparations for the plaza—the impor-tant ones—those last steps that bring the bulls and the killers of bulls into the ring. The bulls are what I'd like to think of now.

Taking our example from a first-class bull ring, the toros are generally brought by road to the plaza, at least twenty-four hours before the corrida. Each bull is loaded, with the help of steers, into a small, individual pen—or *cajón*—for its own and its companions' safety. A conventional corrida usually calls for six bulls to be killed by three matadors. For first-class rings, two reserve bulls are also required to be supplied; for less exalted rings, only one is required. At the plaza, these eight bulls are let loose into a corral where they are examined by three vets to see if they have any defects of trapío, any obvious health or temperamental problems. At first-class rings they are also checked to see if they are of sufficient weight. Less well-equipped, and sensibly cautious, rings weigh the bulls after death.

On the morning of the corrida there is another veterinary examination to see if any weaknesses or difficulties have developed overnight. After this examination, the *sorteo* takes place. This is the process whereby the six principal bulls are paired (often a weaker with a stronger) to try and produce some equality of form and performance throughout the afternoon. This pairing is decided, sometimes in long and heated discussions, between representatives of the matadors—customarily the apoderados and the *banderilleros de confianza*. The banderillero de confianza is generally an older, experienced torero who acts as a kind of combined coach, caddy and psychotherapist to the matador. Once the pairings have been made, the names and numbers of the three pairs are written on pieces of paper, rolled up and thrown into a hat. The pairs are then drawn and allotted in order of the matadors' seniority: top of the bill last. The bulls are then moved into separate pens by an ingenious system of gates and latches and left undisturbed. They will not now be fed before the corrida. Matadors almost never attend the sorteo, they would rather not see the bulls before they meet them in the plaza.

Lorca's friend the matador Ignacio Sánchez Mejías did not go to sorteos. Then, unfit, ageing and back in the ring after a considerable absence, Mejías found himself on the way to fight in Manzanares on 11 August 1934. This was, coincidentally, where he had announced his retiral almost exactly seven years before. This was also where the sorteo came to him. He arrived late at the hotel and found the afternoon's other two matadors waiting for him with the hat holding the sorteo lots. So Sánchez Mejías had no choice but to draw out his own choice of bulls. Later that day, one of the pair would kill him.

And this is the story of the conventional steps taken to bring the bull to the plaza, but—of course—other, less conventional preparations are also made. Ill-informed animal rights activists will mention the mythical stuffing-up of bull's nostrils with cotton wool before the corrida (which would be counter-productive and laughably easy to spot), the sprinkling of chloroform on capes (which might well knock out the matador), and the sandbagging of bulls in the kidney area, which would be harder to spot, but would become rather obvious in the ring and the later veterinary examination. Sadly, the activists are not so familiar with the abuses which are actually perpetrated.

Aficionados are much more familiar with bull-rigging and certainly accept the widespread corruption of the corrida, the kind of bad faith designed to save matadors' lives, or to get men with broken nerves, or failing abilities, into the ring with enough faith in themselves to get them through the afternoon. It is, of course, the kind of bad faith which makes the image of an honourable, unchanging, inviolable corrida—also familiar among some aficionados—a remarkable example of romantic self-deception.

It is generally agreed that, since Belmonte and "Joselito" awakened the public's appetite for closer and closer encounters between the toro and the matador, breeders have been encouraged to produce more and more docile bulls. The measures of this docility are all relative, but a ganadero whose bulls are constantly rejected by every matador with any pull will very likely get the hint and start to calm his bloodline down.

This slightly less savage bull may be rendered even less dangerous by a sudden burst of feeding before he reaches the plaza which causes him to put on weight, but not muscle. Obviously a fat bull will be perfectly healthy, but will tire easily and be more manageable in the final, close-quarter stages of the corrida. An under-age bull—say a three-year-old in a first-class ring—can be fattened to look like a four-year-old. Bulls may also be doped, but this is fairly easy to spot—and corrida crowds are not slow to point out a groggy-looking bull and call for a replacement. Doping relies on a surprising amount of guesswork to produce a dose which actually works but isn't debilitating. It would also tend to be picked up by the regulation post-mortem. In smaller rings, bulls may be disorientated by being left in their cajóns which are then up-ended slightly, leaving the bulls head-down. This produces the effect of doping without the need for chemical intervention.

The most effective and widespread method of weakening a bull involves simply feeding it salt—which it adores and will consume in impressive quantities. The salt-gorged bull is then kept thirsty for a period and, once it is allowed water, it can easily drink enough to produce a massively purgative effect. Obviously, this kind of digestive upset, close to the time of the corrida, significantly weakens the bull.

This and other *trucos*—or tricks—produce the overall effect described below by Joaquín Vidal, *El País'* long-established, moderately reclusive and famously incorruptible corrida correspondent.

"I still insist that I don't believe the falling down of toros is caused by a lack of casta. Let me explain. Take a milk cow. Nothing could be more lacking in casta than a milk cow! Let this cow out into a ring, and it won't fall down. It will moo, jump into the *callejón*,* throw itself down on the ground even, but it won't fall down. The collapse of toros is common, constant, almost without exception, it happens in just about every plaza, and it doesn't come from a lack of casta. It is a fraud!"†

The last and most famous truco is horn-shaving, or *afeitar*. This involves restraining, and therefore stressing, the bull, giving it a more or less ineffective sedative and then taking a, usually electric, saw to the ends of its horns. Between one and two inches will be removed before the horn is then painstakingly—and often painfully—filed, sanded, polished and dyed to resemble an unadulterated horn. Even the great matador Domingo Ortega admitted that horn-shaving was customary on his ganadería in the 1950s and the practice has by no

---

*The narrow passage between the barrera which surrounds the ring and the wall which fronts the first row of audience seating.
†From *Toros*, a fortnightly French taurine magazine.

means fallen out of use. The bulls of Victorino Martín are said to be the only ones guaranteed to remain unshaven.

The shaving itself disturbs the bull, may cause it continuing pain if the cut was made too deep, and throws the animal off when it comes to use horns which are now a length it is unused to. Sometimes, observers can pick up shaving—perhaps fluid or blood will ooze from the horn tips, perhaps their shine will be unconvincing, perhaps the horn ends will tend to splinter and split when they impact against the wooden *barrera.** Sometimes, the fraud is harder to spot and vets, if they even suspect tampering in the first place, will have to send horn cross-sections away to be analysed microscopically before they can be sure the horns have been altered.

There are arguments about how effective afeitar is in disabling a bull, but its widespread use—if nothing else—would tend to suggest that it produces the desired effect. Inches or fractions of inches taken out of the diameter of a hooking move might mean the difference between life and death. Nevertheless, a shaved horn is still hard, still dangerous, still at the front of half a ton of force. The stress and confusion to which afeitar subjects a bull may produce the sort of cautious and unpredictable behaviour which can be fatal to matadors. "Manolete" was killed by a bull with shaved horns.

If nothing else, afeitar produces a kind of faith in the matador, a little extra something that may send him into

---

*The wooden barrier which surrounds the bull ring.

the ring with more assurance, that may allow him to perform at full stretch.

I'm thinking a lot about faith today, being far from any of my own—the kind of faith that can lead a person out into their life, into their voice, their vocation, the kind that accompanies human beings as they come close to their deaths, to the plaza's sand, to the moment that lifts, that waits for God.

I've left the Plaza Mayor and come down to the Calle de la Fé, a cramped little street, currently as grey and rain-washed as the rest of Madrid. The calle cuts a thin path up past various bars, a hairdresser's, a cake shop and ends its climb before a bulbously ugly church. The street was the Calle Sinagoga—Synagogue Street— before Madrid's Jews were expelled in 1492. The synagogue was destroyed and has been replaced by a place of Christian worship ever since. Which is when the calle got its new name, the unconsciously ironic Street of Faith. Moors and Jews who converted, so the story goes, were forced to walk barefoot here, to climb as far as the church and be baptised—willingness to undergo public humiliation and suffering being taken as a good indicator of conversion to Christianity.

To walk away from life as a refugee by walking away from your God—I can't guess what kind of faith that might involve, the very frail or the impregnably certain.

I walk up the Street of Faith and back, find it only slightly depressing, the cold gnawing in my neck. If there's any blasphemy happening here today, it's my intrusion—a person who simply abandoned their faith under quite commonplace duress, a person who will look at anything.

Back in my hotel room I have a tiny plaster model I bought in Granada for good luck. It takes the form of a walking figure, hooded and robed in scarlet. Which is to say, a figure wearing the traditional costume of one of the many socially influential lay "brotherhoods" who parade—a torchlit reminder of the Inquisition's beauties—along with Catholic icons on holy days in a number of Spanish cities. Across the bottom of the model is the word *Rescate.* I don't even know what this means, but suspect it may not be anything in my favour. I recall that Lorca, in a fit of piety, or guilt, petitioned to join one of these associations and almost undoubtedly marched with them once, perhaps looking for the benefits of penance, pilgrimage, the salvation in a walk of faith.

Which brings me to the matador and the adrenaline-scented morning of the corrida. While the bull is being brought to the plaza, examined, selected, left alone in a quiet pen, the killer of bulls also prepares. He takes his first steps on the path that can only take him to the sand of the ring, the plaza's test of his good fortune, his faith in himself, his skill.

Outside the Las Ventas bull ring in Madrid there are a variety of statues. One shows a matador saluting Alexander Fleming for his achievements in antisepsis, and another features a simple wooden chair, over which is draped the traje de luces, the matador's traditional fighting costume. The chair makes an unfamiliar icon, both threatening and domestic. The chair is where it begins.

The matador may spend his morning as he wishes, trying to idle anonymously in the streets outside his hotel, perhaps managing to eat, perhaps attempting to doze as he's driven from yesterday's plaza and heads for today's. But, perhaps while the matador snatches a last half-sleep before the business of the day takes hold, there will always come a point when the sword boy or *mozo de espada* sets out the traje de luces, draped in strict order over a chair. The ritual of the corrida opens with the traje de luces, with the putting on of vestments, if you like. The tight, uncomfortable, complicated and deeply symbolic matador's costume can only be donned with assistance (usually from at least the mozo) in a process which takes something like an hour.

In one of a succession of hotel rooms, a man strips off his everyday self and slowly clothes himself in the corrida. Which may sound overly dramatic, but this is the moment when the matador can no longer avoid consideration of the coming afternoon's trial. Whatever the matador's level of conventionally religious faith, he will have his own accretion of good luck charms, holy images and tokens. Often a small, portable altar sits in the room, witness to each preparation, each internal and external transformation.

I'm told that Enrique Ponce, currently Spain's top-ranking matador, is a serious and intelligent man, not given to irrationality in his everyday life. Nevertheless, his peregrinations from plaza to plaza are always accompanied by a huge altar, covered in an increasing collection of talismans, cards and candles, each of which is displayed in a particular order, touched in a particular order before he leaves for his work.

It is, naturally, a great honour to be invited to the dressing of a matador, to see the start of his transition from one world to another. In the corrida's world where love and respect are so often tinged with an appetite for celebrity, a voyeur's desire for possession, journalists, aficionados and friends may all jostle about the matador as he becomes himself, the self he only finds in the plaza. It is quite acceptable to watch a man rendered speechless by the closing of his concentration on an unseen, but anticipated object, the heat of an unknown life, energy without intelligence, instinct pursued and pursuing without compassion, the bull.

Although the traje de luces is little changed since the sixteenth century, its current form is said to owe much to Goya, the eighteenth-century painter and sometime torero. Goya, the artist who portrayed four Spanish kings, dramatic corridas and baroque obscenities. Goya, the man questioned by the Inquisition whose later work shows blurring landscapes of madness and torture, desolate faces and eyes filled with animal pain, or an utter emptiness. *Goyescos*, quaintly historical corridas, are still held in his honour—they seek to re-create his costumes rather than his later paintings, of course. But I can't help seeing the twist of helplessly displayed sacrifice in both.

So the matador puts on his trade's history with his traje, the uniform of his calling, a sheath of superstition over his skin. He begins with pink (no one quite knows why pink) silk stockings, two pairs, each smoothed up and over the calf and secured with elastic garters. It seems suitably absurd that in this stylishly dangerous world, stocking wrinkles should be a legitimate concern. Like military men, matadors are meant to die in good order.

And good order is in the details. Matadors usually tape the penis in place against the root and side of the thigh. Any padding added at this point is, naturally, of more psychological than actual benefit, although it may help to make the extremely tight fit of the traje's britches rather more bearable. This snug fit, of course, has the effect of displaying the matador's gender more than eloquently, at which point the padding may provide a certain ego-boost. Aficionados joke about "one-handkerchief" and "two-handkerchief" matadors. Very occasionally, a horn rip to the matador's clothing may be more than usually revealing. Morenito de Maracay was informally elected by some aficionados as Torero's Most Outstanding Man after one such incident a few years ago. Beyond the obvious innuendo and machismo, Maracay's embarrassment serves as a reminder of how prevalent inner-thigh injuries are in the corrida. It's by no means unheard of for matadors to lose testicles as a result of such wounds.

Over whatever personal arrangements the matador favours, comes the underwear: traditionally anachronistic knee-length underpants. Occasionally these have been replaced by full-length leotards, in which case the stockings are fastened over them.

Next, the *talleguilla*—the miraculously tight embroidered silk britches of the traje. These may be in almost any colour, although almost every shade—if not every traje—has its good and bad luck stories. It is, perhaps, unsurprising that yellow, the colour of the *sanbenito*, still has a particularly evil reputation, particularly among gypsy toreros. Some matadors will even replace the yellow lining of the capote de brega with blue. Loaned suits may bring death to the borrower, red (it is wrongly suggested) may lead the bull to confuse the man with the red muleta. Characteristically, Julián López López—"El Juli"—the young phenomenon astonishing Spanish aficionados at the moment, favours a red suit.

The talleguilla is tight, in the manner of fencer's britches, and for much the same reasons. There must be no possibility of the bull's horns snagging a loose piece of cloth and so catching and wounding the matador. Fear, exertion and, in summer, the concentrated heat of a ring will sweat pounds off the matador during the corrida and leave the suit relatively, but still not dangerously, loose. It takes a great deal of time and assistance to ease the man into his talleguilla—some even straddle a rolled towel and are jogged into their britches in tiny jolts. Many toreros say that it takes years for a man to get over the sense of absolute exposure that the talleguilla can inspire in the wearer. From roughly nipple height to just below the knee, they seem to both trap and reveal his body.

The talleguilla is fastened below the knee, either with drawstrings or, less traditionally, with elastic, and tassels called—of course—*machos* are precisely positioned at the edge of the talleguilla on the outside of the leg.

Next, the matador's *zapatillas*—the flat, black slippers which give all but the most graceful a characteristic, slightly flat-footed gait. The slippers appear an illogically insubstantial choice of footwear, even in a tradition where self-protection is often synonymous with dishonour. The soles of the zapatillas are, in fact, more resilient than appearances might suggest and are ribbed for grip. Even so, when fighting in the rain (almost all rings are open-air) matadors may choose to proceed in stocking feet, to prevent potentially fatal slipping, and can then make a sorry spectacle, wet-headed, their suit blurred with blood and water, their stockings in shreds at the feet.

Next, the *coleta*. This is the false pigtail worn by all toreros, except the picador, as a mark of their profession. Until Belmonte cut off his coleta in an attempt to render himself less recognisable in the street, these pigtails were simply a permanent part of any given torero's coiffeur. Since Belmonte, false coletas—or *añadidos*—often made of sweetheart's or mother's hair—have been fixed to the head under a plain, rounded button so that they just show below the matador's hat, the *montera*. The official retirement ritual of the matador is still the "cutting" of the coleta.

Next, the matador puts on a ruffle-fronted linen shirt and fastens his braces. He puts on his narrow black tie— the *corbatín*—which is secured to his shirt with a stitch of thread. The tie gives an incongruously schoolboy effect, a reminder that matadors begin their careers as very young men and that their dreams are even younger. Once a sash has been fastened very securely around the talleguilla, the matador is ready for his jacket.

The *chaquetilla*, or jacket, is a stiff, heavy affair, once again of silk and embroidery which will only reach to something like the depth of the man's shoulder blades. Its colour will match that of the talleguilla. Traditionally, only matadors have the right to wear gold embroidery on their whole traje. Picadors may have gold on their jackets, but their trousers are of buckskin. The banderilleros may wear black, white or silver embroidery. For freedom of movement, the jacket's sleeves are attached by laces only at the top of the shoulder, this join being covered by ornately embroidered epaulettes.

The montera finishes the matador's costume. This is a solid, weighty hat, covered with long-napped black velour reminiscent of animal fur. It has changed in shape over the centuries from a type of topknot, to an unwieldy-looking pyramidical structure burdened with black frogging, to the deep, winged skull-cap of today. The montera is worn during the initial cape passes in the ring. It is removed for the kill and sometimes used to dedicate the death of the bull, either to a particular, forewarned audience member or to the crowd as a whole. Only a promising bull will be dedicated in a *brindis*, or toast, the best type of animal being reserved for the audience. The audience may then reciprocate by rewarding a good performance with requests that the matador be granted either one or two of the bull's ears—matadors are ranked by the number of ears—and, more vulgarly and recently, tails—that they cut in a season.

If the brindis is for the crowd, the matador will swivel round, holding the montera above his head in salute; he will then throw it over his shoulder to land, either right-side-up or not, on the sand. There are, naturally, superstitions regarding this point. If the montera lands upside-down it is most often said to lie open and waiting to hold the matador's blood. To allay this anxiety, a quieter rival tradition states that, had the montera landed the opposite way, it could have been considered to be spilling his luck. Some matadors will tip the montera over if its gape disturbs them, or simply place it as they would like. The montera is removed for the kill as a sign of respect, primarily to the bull. Very occasionally a senior matador who feels he is facing an inadequate bull will signal his displeasure by killing it without removing his montera.

The matador will also carry a lavishly embroidered parade cape—the *capote de paseo*—as he first processes into the ring. This will be wrapped around him, sling-fashion in the time-honoured manner, and may bear images of the matador's patron saint.

The traje de luces itself costs something approaching three thousand dollars and can weigh a little in excess of one stone. The jacket, in particular, is exceptionally stiff, partly with embroidery and partly because of the rather rudimentary care to which it is subjected. During the corrida, the traje will be spattered, if not daubed, with bull's blood and impregnated with sweat. It can only be cleaned by holding it under running water and scrubbing with soap and a hard brush.

Once in his traje, the matador will set his mind, perform his private acts of faith. Then he will start his journey to the ring. A burning, glistening image in silk and metal thread, he will appear walking quietly, perhaps slipping between admirers and autograph-hunters, into the toreros' entrance to the plaza. This is where the comfort and the delight of his vocation have led. This is where he's on his own. Back in the hotel room there may well be a candle, left burning for his sake.

Chapter Six

Self-Portrait

Sunday, 27th September, Las Ventas, Madrid. Under a watery sun, the plaza fills for today's corrida and I am already in my seat. Although by seat I mean my numbered space on one of the long, grey stone benches that circle the ring, interrupted, here and there, by narrow sets of steps. Built to hold 23,000, this is unmistakably an arena in the Roman style, but it's a brick and rust-stained concrete affair with no more charm or menace than a shopping centre wrapped up in a mildly Moorish façade. Here, as in all other plazas, the cheapest seats are the "*Sol*"—on the side of the ring which catches, in high summer, the truly murderous sun—"*Sombre*"—the expensive shaded arc where the President's box is situated and, therefore, where the matador will wish to display his best work—and "*Sol y Sombre*"—the mid-price, compromise section, not too far from the action and not unremittingly sun-baked, should there be any sun to speak of. There is very little today, but at least it isn't actually raining. My seat is "*Sol y Sombre,*" and almost exactly faces the toril gate, also poetically known as the Gate of Fear—the bull's entrance to the ring.

My knees are unavoidably pressed into the upper back of the man seated in front of me, while an unavoidable pair of knees is, likewise, pressed into my upper back, courtesy of the row behind, and both my elbows are nipped in by, to my left, a well-dressed Madrid woman of middle age and, to my right, a young man in a T-shirt and baseball cap. My spine is starting to smart and I am regretting my stupidly Calvinist choice to forgo the hire of a cushion. The rigid chill of the masonry has already crept up as far as my hips.

Still, the gentle crush around me is surprisingly amiable. There is a pre-theatre, rather than a pre-match, atmosphere. People stand to wave at friends; there is a fair amount of laughter, melodious chat. Closest to the ring, in the best *barrera* and *contra-barrera*, ringside seats, there are the unmistakably rich, already thickly wreathed in cigar smoke: all immaculate haircuts and expensively white teeth, shoulders draped in cashmere sweaters, or tinily freighted with pointless handbags. The Sol section is dotted with little groups of smart twentysomethings, snug couples and a high proportion of barrel-chested older men with short necks and cloth caps. Ushers wearing gold-braided peaked caps, but making no other efforts towards a uniform, direct people to their correct numbered segment of the *tendido*—the "slopes" of seats, reaching from the barrera to the high *gradas*, the balconies. The band, a wild handful of mariachi brass, wails into a practice burst of apparently drunken life, running through a few of its paso dobles. Most of these tunes are written specially for the corrida and may take their names from great matadors or plazas.

From above me, paper money is passed down from row to row until it reaches a vendor at the foot of the tendido who renders up, in return, a palmful of change and a glass of whisky. Both are duly delivered back to their intended recipient, entirely unscathed. In fact, on all sides money, ice creams and soft drinks are being transported up and down the arena. I try to imagine anything similar even being attempted in Britain. And then, before the ceremony begins, I consider the order of service.

The corrida is divided into three acts—the *tercios* or *suertes*—and a prologue. The prologue is the *paseíllo*, a parade involving all the human participants of the corrida. First, mounted and plushly costumed in the feathered hats and velvet of the sixteenth century, come one or two constables. The constable—*alguacil*—is the President's representative in the ring. It is the alguacil who officially asks permission for the corrida to begin by doffing his hat. The President answers by waving a white handkerchief. As the band plays a paso doble, the constables lead in the matadors—three of them in a standard corrida—who walk, glistening capotes de paseo draped over their shining trajes de luces, with the cuadrillas in single file behind them. The most senior matador is to the right—as the President views things— the next senior to the left and the junior in the middle. The peones—the teams of three banderilleros—in their slightly more modest trajes and capotes, lead the cuadrillas. Then come the three pairs of mounted picadors in their gold-braided jackets and wide, slightly comic beaver hats, their feet and shins encased in steel armour to stave off all but the most penetrating horns. Their horses are blindfolded and wrapped round in heavy padding—the *peto*—which protects the flanks and belly. Behind them come the reserve picadors and the picadors' aides, the *monosabios*, or "wise monkeys," men on foot, dressed vaguely like janitors, who are—somewhat perversely—named after a troupe of nineteenth-century tumblers, who were in their turn somewhat connected to a troupe of monkeys. Next come a number of carpenters, who repair the barrera when necessary, and the sand-levellers who tend to the arena. Appropriately, the last to appear are the mule drivers and their teams who will drag out the bull's bodies as the business of the day progresses. The mule's harness is decorated with bells.

When all the above have saluted the President, much as gladiators would have saluted the senior dignitary present in a Roman ring, they make a leisurely circuit of the sand while the band plays. The alguacil passes the toril gate key to the designated attendant and then all but the matadors and their cuadrillas leave. Now, before the gate is opened and the bull enters, the toreros remove their capotes de paseo and drape them over the barrera. The toreros then unfold their capotes de brega, the broad, magenta silk capes with, usually, a yellow percale lining. They make a few practice passes but do nothing that might be called—dishonourable thought—a warm-up.

Next the broad toril gate swings heavily and impressively open and the bull enters, hooves possibly thundering. There is an airless moment while the audience and toreros assess the bull. Now, for a brief period, depending partly on the bull's and the matador's temperament, the bull will be tested with the capotes. The matador who is to kill this first bull will watch his peones entice it to chase dragged capes, trying to discern the animal's form. He will also play it with cape passes based around the *veronica*. The veronica pass, invented by "Costillares," involves holding the cape up in front of the body with both hands, allegedly in the manner of Saint Veronica when she held a cloth to mop the face of Christ on his way to Calvary. The parallels between one man on his way to certain death and another doing his best to avoid it make for the kind of symbolism in which the corrida delights. Veronica's cloth, stained with blood and sweat, is considered by some to be the first self-portrait. What follows in the corrida, also stained with blood and sweat, forms another self-portrait, both particular and general—one of fear and faith, luck and skill, pain cut close to joy—the lines a vocation can score across a life.

When this series of exploratory passes is over, the signal from the President's white handkerchief heralds the first act of the corrida proper. This is the *Suerte de Varas*, the Act of the Spears. In this act, the two picadors enter again and, standing within carefully marked lines towards the edge of the ring, each "tests the bull's mettle," much as it was tested once before in the tientas on the ganadería. Each picador is armed with a long wooden pole, the *vara* which terminates in the *puya*. This is a spike tipped with a 29mm pyramid of cutting steel, preceded by 30mm of cord-wrapped steel and then a steel crosspiece, designed to stop the vara from piercing the bull too deeply. The idea is that the picador should induce the bull to charge him and then catch the animal behind the morrillo with the vara. The spine should not be damaged, the vara should not be removed and then slyly replaced within the same wound to increase its severity, and nor should the flesh be ripped. This is intended to be a matter of courteous injury, controlled by the kind of etiquette an Inquisitor would recognise and the desire to leave the bull relatively mobile for the next two acts.

In the days when the horse was not protected with padding, any failure of the picador to deflect and then arrest the bull's charge would probably mean death by disembowelment for the horse and a dangerous tumble for the picador. In effect, it is almost impossible for the picador to do his job and defend his horse without his role coming much closer to that of the more mobile and energetic rejoneador. The introduction of the peto by Royal Decree in 1928 means that plazas are no longer regularly littered with horse corpses, but remains a bone of great contention with some purist aficionados. It is believed in some quarters that horse-killing greatly improves the bull's "spirit" for the remainder of its time in the ring and is the only fit proof of its "bravery." Some will even claim that horse's blood on the bull's horns helped to prevent infection if they later pierced a man. This is obviously nonsense—"El Tato,"* for example, lost his leg to gangrene after a *cornada* was contaminated with horse's blood. Arguments are cited which state, reasonably enough, that the blindfolded and terri-

---

*There is currently a matador of that name, but I refer to his predecessor who did attempt a return to the ring with a prosthetic leg but, tears running down his face, was forced to admit defeat. His leg was put on display in a Madrid shopfront for many years until it was destroyed in a fire.

fied horse is currently buffeted by massive impacts, suffering great stress and possibly broken bones. Aficionados, condemning this equine suffering as unacceptable, often recommended a return to the "kinder" option of evisceration, rather than the strict application of rules which might forbid the picador from allowing the bull to broadside his horse and then simply leaning in with the vara while the bull is relatively preoccupied with shoving against the peto and the flank beneath. Obviously, the best option for the horse would be its removal from the ring or, at least, an entirely different style of horsemanship. This is unlikely, although the early corridas for novilleros are customarily held without picadors. Among many aficionados there seems to remain a strong and mainly irrational desire for the bull to prove his killing ability in the ring with the unwitting assistance of one or more horses. Any interest in human injury is much more firmly sublimated.

There are meant to be two or three encounters—*puyazos*—between the bulls and the picador's lances: the President may reduce the number if the bull seems to be bearing up particularly badly. Between the puyazos, each of the matadors will draw the bull away into a series of passes. And so begins the tempering of the bull's natural instincts into the governed movements of an interaction between the animal, the cape and the man. The three principles of toreo are *parar, mandar, templar*—to stand one's ground, to completely dominate and control the bull, and to govern the pace of all its actions, maintaining a fixed distance between the cloth and the bull's horns. These three principles begin to be put into operation here. This leads to the fourth ideal of toreo, *cargar la suerte*, an untranslatable phrase which might be rendered as "to be true to the soul of the corrida."

Although the Suerte de Varas was once used to display the aristocratic skill of the mounted man and the highly trained horse, it now mainly serves to quieten the bull and to lower its head. This is vital for the next two stages of the corrida, when men will approach the bull, reaching directly over its passing horns. If the head is high, it will be impossible to reach over it and make the kill. There may also be an increased risk of receiving a cornada through the heart. This risk of death is at the core of the corrida's honour code—this potential bartering of life for life is central to its logic. Any manoeuvres which seek to fake or avoid this exposure are regarded with contempt.

It is typical of the corrida that this contempt is moderated with respect for the dangers of the torero's trade and the realities of terror. At the opposite extreme, apparently suicidal risk-taking is admired, but with a certain reservation—it can smack, after all, of pride, or the kind of self-confidence which either changes the accepted order of the corrida, or removes it and opens the way for too much death. And there's nothing like the death of a well-loved torero for showing the aficionado an uncomfortable self-portrait: pointing up the voyeurism, the non-combatant's pedantry, the appetite for dangerous excellence in the corrida's audience.

In the *Suerte de Banderillas*, three pairs of banderillas will be driven into the bull's back. Usually the banderillas will be placed by the peones and a very few banderilleros may become famous in their own right for their bravery and skill. Rising on tiptoe, holding "the sticks" aloft, the men then dart in towards the charging bull and drive the banderillas into the area around the morrillo, just as they dodge aside from the animal's path and the closing curve of its horn. The two most recent corrida deaths—in 1992—involved banderilleros, both of whom took cornadas in their hearts. Occasionally, matadors may place their own banderillas, although this is now quite uncommon. Notably, "El Juli," the young phenomenon, often acts as his own banderillero, earning the, occasionally slightly anxious, admiration of his audiences. Particularly foolhardy toreros may use "short" banderillas, breaking off part of the shaft before they place them, thus forcing themselves to bring their bodies much closer to the bull's horns. This practice is now pretty much unheard of.

Black banderillas, particularly heavily barbed darts, are used as a sign of disrespect for the bull's condition and as a criticism of the ganadero—the bull is punished for the man's faults as a breeder. It is no longer legal to use gunpowder banderillas—*banderillas de fuego*—on a bull without casta, in an effort to liven up, humiliate, or quite simply dement the animal, sending it plunging around the ring, shoulders trailing a pall of smoke and sparks. Just as each suerte is heralded by a white handkerchief, so the use of black banderillas is signalled by a black handkerchief. Should a bull prove lacking in spirit at any stage of the corrida, the President's display of a green handkerchief will bring about its expulsion from the ring and the disgrace of the ganadería. This disgrace seems to last approximately as long as similar public disapproval shown towards, say, wife-slapping footballers, or drug-abusing sprinters, which is to say, for hardly any time at all.

The purpose of the Suerte de Banderillas is slightly foggy—beyond its display of human agility and nerve, the shiver in the instant when a man poises barbed darts above his head in an elegantly vicious parody of horns. A variety of expert opinions claim that the accurate place-ment of the banderillas will correct a tendency in the bull to hook to one side, something which, in actuality, many matadors say is untrue. Banderillas are also claimed to brighten a bull after the sapping effect of the puya, although how six small stab wounds could remedy sev-eral larger ones is beyond me. What is unquestionable is that, after this stage, the bull is generally slower still and holds its head yet lower.

This progression of the bull from relative good health to bloodied exhaustion during the corrida is also sum-marised in three stages, from *levantado*, when the bull is unharmed, normally alert and easily tricked, to *parado* when he is more tired and cautious, wounded and liable to time his attacks carefully with a kind of desperate concentration, to *aplombado* when he is leaden, low-headed, swollen-tongued, unwilling to charge and liable to chop with his horns. Once he is aplombado, he is very close to being killed. Once he is aplombado, this would seem to be a mercy.

And, when the President signals again, the *Suerte de Matar* begins, the Act of the Kill. This is more usually known as the *faena*—what has increasingly become the heart of the corrida as simple preparations for a kill have grown more and more elaborate and artistic. Once the white handkerchief has been shown, the matador bares his head and officially asks permission to kill the bull. He will then, should he wish, dedicate the bull's death in a brindis. Individuals who have received a dedication, taking the matador's montera into their temporary safe-keeping for the duration of the kill, are expected to reciprocate with a gift, perhaps placing a few folded notes of money into the hat when they give it back. Some offerings can, however, be more unexpected and generous, running to banquets and expensive art works. Enrique Ponce was, for example, invited to go shooting with King Juan Carlos in recompense for a brindis—he'd anticipated something more along the lines of a signed photograph.

The formalities over, a particularly taut silence falls and the matador begins to play the bull with the small, red serge cape: the muleta. This egg-shaped cape is spread and fixed over a short dowel and, when held in the right hand, is extended even further by the blade of the matador's sword. This means that left-hand passes allow the bull to come closer to the man's body than the right-handed variety. In the faena, the matador aims to wind the bull's charges closer and closer around himself, to link chains of passes in different directions and to make the bull appear, at some level, "comfortable" with the process of charging, as a peculiar rapport seems to form between man, animal and observers. If the matador is performing especially well (in any plaza other than Las Ventas) the President will signal that the band should play paso dobles while the suerte progresses and a curious, intense dance between two species will begin, as blood wells out of the bull's wounds and is brushed across the legs, stomach and chest of the matador with each tight slip and turn of the bull against him.

At the end of this suerte, the bull can manage hardly a step more, and stands sunken-headed, shoulders bright with gore, flanks heaving. Now the matador prepares for the Moment of Truth, the kill. Most modern matadors carry a fake, light aluminium sword with them during the Suerte de Matar and then go to the barrera when the time has come to kill. There the mozo de espada is waiting with the real, slightly curved steel blade. Another name for the matador is *espada*, a blade.

In an icy stillness, the matador now walks towards his animal. He makes it follow the cloth only until it seems settled and has halted with its head down and its feet apart and, therefore, its shoulder blades open. The matador then withdraws a few feet away and "cites" the animal. The pose is strange, atavistic, entirely concerned with killing and with the bull. Right leg locked straight behind him, left bent forward with the heel raised, the man holds muleta low in his left hand, raises the sword in his right and stares along its blade towards the waiting bull. At this point the matador's face changes, fixes in a killing grimace, a kind of death mask. Then, moving in at tremendous speed, the matador simultaneously lures the bull's head down and to the right with the muleta and goes in over the head to plunge the sword, hopefully into the bull's rubio, and then draw back, unharmed, as the horn passes, the animal's head lifts, beyond him, as its body begins to sink and die. This final succession of moves means that the matador must make the sign of the cross with his arms, in order to move the bull's head and horns as he needs, so that he can kill and survive.

Having offered his life close to the horn, he kills the bull. Death balanced against death, absolute loss against absolute loss: this, in the corrida, constitutes truth.

The bull is then dragged out by the mule team, while the sand-levellers smooth any irregularities the three tercios have left in the arena's surface and scoop up the bloodstained sand. If the bull has done well it will be dragged once round the ring, limp head jolting, and applauded with genuine warmth. If the matador has done well, he may be granted his own lap of honour. To this, with reference to the resident experts who advise the President, may be added the presentation of one, or two, of the dead bull's ears and perhaps the tail—these are then usually given away to fans. The ultimate accolade would incorporate the receipt of two ears and then being lifted aloft and carried in triumph out of the principal gate of the plaza. Each of these awards is in the gift of the President, although the crowd will always petition hard for its favourites and wave encouraging white handkerchiefs to sway the official opinion. Contrary to popular belief, matadors do not customarily feast on the testicles of their victims. Given that a well-ranked matador might kill enough bulls in a week to produce around fifty of these sizeable delicacies, the sheer volume of supply alone might well be off-putting.

There are other variations on the corrida theme. A rejoneador might join the matadors on the bill, or two matadors might take on three bulls apiece, in which case, the pair of "rivals" will be expected to drive each other to new heights of artistry and daring. A great matador may be contracted to kill all the day's six toros—something which is not only physically and emotionally demanding, but also a test of imagination. The matador will have to attempt to make each kill different, sometimes with temperamentally similar bulls from the same ganadería. He will have to please the audience with an afternoon shaped around a succession of novel pass combinations and, almost undoubtedly, an escalation of risk. Rumours suggest that "El Juli" will soon attempt to face seven bulls in two different plazas within the course of one day—which is to say that he intends to confront his own mortality fourteen times within the space of less than twenty-four hours. Given that he often places his own "sticks," this marathon could potentially involve him facing a cornada on a minimum of fifty-six occasions. At this level, the life of the matador must be governed by the same dark mathematics which calculates a soldier's ability to tolerate combat: so many months in a tour of duty, so many missions flown, and mental change, mental trauma, becomes a statistical inevitability. But in the corrida, the matador is not exposed to physical and emotional damage by duty, or conscription—he is a volunteer, a true believer, a lover with his love. And there are no limits to love, it is quite merciless.

All of which is the theory. I'm here with the fact. As the paseíllo ends and the toreros, stiff-limbed, are left in a nervous cluster, alone in the wide space of the ring, the corrida is about to begin in earnest. The capotes de brega are unfurled, refolded and then hugged to the toreros' bodies in what seems a gesture of painful unease. The novilleros—Samuel López, Juan Contreras and Otto Rodríguez—look astonishingly young, thin-lipped, pale, earnestly intent. Their capotes de brega seem too big for them, like bright, hampering blankets. The day seems suddenly colder.

And before I write out the afternoon's catalogue of injury and death—something that even the best words can never entirely approach—I will give you my brindis, my last effort at a *quid pro quo* to balance the ultimate, bodily commitment the plaza requires of animal and man. You already have the death of my vocation, but this is the death I would give you, this good death.

The night I walk out with my Grandfather into the sharp, high black of a winter night. We've spent the whole day together, much as we always did when I was a child: talking, buying sweets in Woolworth's, although neither of us eats sweets anymore, strolling in town with our arms locked, or our palms closed, each to the other's, fingers laced, or only our sides nudging softly, checking we're both still here. The first man I loved to touch, my Grandfather.

We've played cribbage for most of the afternoon and he has cheated, has beaten me hollow with no sign of mercy, no trace of shame. And I've taken his photograph. We never do photograph gladly, he and I, although he always has the knack of elegance when the moment for it comes: the summer snapshot, the family wedding, the small theft of himself. And I never do like to photograph people, to play the thief. But today we've gone against our natures and I've used up most of a film while he's tilted his head and his hands, a retired chargehand tool-setter with a matinee idol's grace, and I've known again that this is the best voice, the finest haircut, the right smile for any man, before our eyes meet through the lens and make us afraid, make us have to stop. Because today he has quietly told me that he is tired of being ill, of being tired, and that he now intends to die. He will finally agree to a heart valve replacement, although he's already very frail, and then plans to leave himself on the operating table, a clean break. He is saying goodbye. Whatever happens later, this is goodbye. The photographs make his last gift and are terrible and wonderful, because this is goodbye.

And we walk out together at the start of the night, breath taken by the shock of a frost, each of our steps slewing slightly, uncertain on dark ice. We are holding each other to keep from falling, to keep from parting, to keep from being apart. At the corner of the street we stop, embrace and kiss. The kiss is slightly clumsy, slightly shortened. I am wearing a hat against the cold and its brim gets in our way. But if we kiss again, we'll cry. So this is it. Without thinking, I've broken our last kiss, the last of our touch.

For the brindis, it is always required to remove your hat.

The first bull, "Aguador," enters, hooves—just as you might expect—pounding a hollow din out of the sand. He kicks and tosses his head, muscles jumping with animal life in the black gloss of his sides and back. An approving murmur runs around the ring. The peones dart about, apparently panic personified, dodging quickly behind the little wooden screens—the *burladeros*, or "deceivers," because they deceive the bull—four of which are placed evenly round the ring to provide a refuge for the toreros. Somewhere behind me, an American tourist laughs at a particularly hasty retreat. An atmosphere of barely controlled hysteria rises from the ring, these men are not in control.

Still, the Venezuelan Otto Rodríguez tries his best to chain passes around "Aguador's" movements. Straight-legged, he edges towards the bull and attempts, each limb tight, to control the animal's motion, to end each sequence with an adequate *remate*—a finishing, flicking pass which will hopefully fix the bull in place, bewildered, at the end of a series of moves and allow the matador a safe retreat. Each pass comes perilously close to chaos, to collapse.

Quickly, the picadors are signalled in and get to work on the animal, leaning down hard on their varas and drawing a good deal of blood which begins to well thickly over the thin, blood-red *divisa* ribbon, fixed in the bull's morrillo just before it enters the ring. The ribbon identifies "Aguador" as a bull of the Navalrosa ganadería. It is quickly obscured. The capework between pics is slight while the crowd grumbles and then whistles as each picador in turn presses into his work, breaking down the bull to save their matador.

By the end of the picing, the bull stumbles to its knees, struggles up, stands much more still than before. The banderilleros now find it tricky to make him charge them and they place their "sticks" rather gingerly with little response from the audience.

Rodríguez takes the muleta and faces a now sluggish, staggering bull. Again, his work seems always to shiver at the brink of catastrophic failure. He advances his leg behind the muleta to provoke a charge, slips further and further forward, but is rarely able to develop the response he needs. Finally, he takes the killing sword with its special, artery-slicing curve—the *muerte*, the death—and cites for the kill, face pale and anguished. The sword goes in to its hilt for a full *estocada*, but doesn't quite find its mark. The bull stands, sunken-headed, unaware that it is dead. The peones use their capes to back the bull against the barrera and there Rodríguez uses the *estoque de descabellar* or simply the *descabello*, a heavy, straight sword with a metal crosspiece near its tip, to deliver a *coup de grâce* to the bull's neck, severing the spinal cord. The bull drops, as if shot, and Rodríguez walks away, grim-faced.

The second bull, "Cantalobos," charges into the ring, full of a kind of physical optimism, the confidence of young strength. In the opening passes, it catches Samuel López, a young Spaniard of nine years' experience, and bumps him to the ground. The plaza catches its breath with a hiss as the peones rush in and draw the bull away with their capes. Barging by the bull is, naturally, far less damaging than a horn wound, but can still cause serious internal damage, with broken bones and potentially fatal haemorrhages. López draws himself to his feet, trying to gather his composure, apparently only bruised. It becomes plaintively clear that the grace and dignity of the matador is not a given, is only earned with every second spent in the ring—the traje de luces is an unforgiving costume, it can begin to look clownish very easily. López makes a few more passes, apparently calmer, more fixed, and turns the bull over to his picadors.

Who immediately have their revenge. There are cries of *"Basta!"*—enough—from all round the arena as the picadors spear as much danger as they can out of the bull. "Cantalobos" strikes the horses full-on in the peto and then strains his hindquarters, pressing in for flesh, while hooves shift, the picador's metal leggings clatter and the vara penetrates, unlocks the blood. After only two pics, the bull is left, rubber-legged, slowly drifting its head from side to side, its tongue thick. López approaches with the muleta like a shy, fatal boy, the bull charges and falls. Again, López provokes a charge and again the bull stumbles over its own impetus. There are whistles from the crowd, and a kind of controlled fury from López who closes yet again and manages, gently, gently, to sneak the bull's body around his own, to distract it from its injuries, to gather its wits and then leave it with a flick of his sword and the first smile we've seen him break. He returns to the bull, works it, mainly using left-handed passes—the *pase natural*—until the animal is, once more, on its knees and then he goes for the sword. López gentles the bull into the proper stance and goes in for the estocada—the name for both the blade and its stroke. Slowly, the animal subsides, the man keeping him always in sight. There are modest appeals for an ear and he takes his bow, honour restored.

Juan Contreras, a twenty-year-old Spaniard who first fought in '94, looks tangibly petrified. And he has the most lively bull yet, a big, woolly-faced beast, the heaviest of the day at 514 kilos—"Caminante."

The brutal rhythm of the day swings in again as the banderilleros dodge the first charges, the matador steps tentatively into capote work and then the picadors weigh in, straining at their spears, less popular and more heavy-handed than their four predecessors. A roll of dis-content washes the plaza as another bull is left, stagger-ing and urinating helplessly, almost too weak to face the muleta. And I consider all those paragraphs I've read about the powerful body chemicals that stop the pain from traumatic injuries from kicking in too quickly: about the gift of dopamine. I recall the story an old sol-dier told me of meeting a wounded man in India who was sitting and singing quietly—a folk song about a nightingale—apparently unaware that his hat was the only thing holding his head together.

I don't know how much pain the bull is in, nor when its shock may spin into injury, nor even how an animal may "feel" such things, but I do appear to be observing considerable distress—distress which seems to remove the possibility of the corrida's promised artistry ever making an appearance. I also can't help noticing the black joke, winking under it all—the constant portrayal of the innocent entering an unknown world, being pun-ished for its own nature: the greater its promise, the deeper the wounds.

As a banderillero performs a *quite*, a drawing-away of the bull, in this case from the picador, he is suddenly pursued by the animal. The American voice behind me lifts a cheer.

With the muleta, the bull is unsteady but cunning. As its strength pumps out onto the sand, it hooks unex-pectedly, waits for the man. It finally catches Contreras and rips open the leg of his talleguilla. The silk flapping stupidly away from the exposed linen beneath destroys the man's poise but also indicates how close "Caminante's" horns came to ripping open his leg. Now, having worried ineffectually at the fallen man, the bull itself drops and has to be lifted up, cautiously, absurdly, by the peones who tug at its tail and wave their capes. A pool of blood has gathered where it has lain. This is much nearer butchery and farce than art.

Contreras, in a chalky trance, goes in for the stumbling bull and briefly hugs it at the waist, almost leaning on it, feet stumbling for grip. He backs off, fetches his sword, cites tremulously and misses the kill. A sigh gathers in the crowd, seeming to close from far away. Contreras tries again, hooking out the first sword with a new one while a tourist announces, "This sucks." The peones close round the bull, keeping it in position, as Contreras finally gives the descabello.

"Caminante" is dragged away while, in a brief interval, the sand is levelled and the white lines that mark its three zones are renewed. Much of the day's blood is cleared away. Some tourists leave, unhappy. I take one of my larger pills and eat some lemon biscuits, allegedly made by nuns from Alcalá. I have been told that the extraordinarily yellow sand used in the plazas usually comes from Alcalá. The biscuits prove to be appropriately dry and abrasive.

And now Otto Rodríguez is back, kneeling in front of the Gate of Fear in preparation for a manoeuvre which has already stilled the plaza. He hopes to perform a *larga cambiada de rodillas*—a more than averagely insane pass, commonly known as *a porta goyola*—which means the matador has to guess roughly how and where the bull will emerge from the gate, fix himself in a position of virtually immobile vulnerability and then, as the beast first breaks into light, must swing the capote, one-handed over his head and to the side, causing the bull to either crash past him or leap his shoulder. I've heard it said that there is a 50 per cent chance of the man simply having his face kicked in.

Rodríguez shifts a little on his knees, the strain telling, beginning to produce a fatal doubt. But then the bull is out and the pass more or less elegantly completed and the man can walk into the heart of the plaza with a certain buoyancy while "Extremeño" gallops his 506 kilos across alien sand.

His confidence lifted, Rodríguez begins to perform, moves the capote well, fanning and flaring it out into whipping remates, the two-handed *media veronica* which lifts and spins evenly from the matador's waist, and the one-handed *rebolera*, which lashes the capote out at an angle past his body—both of them stop the bull in its tracks, dominated, betrayed by instinct.

The picadors are, if anything, more brutal in their work while the crowd, now with Rodríguez, call out for him to stop the damage. He does indeed draw the groggy animal away into beguiling passes, but its spirit seems broken. It will no longer charge the horses, only stares at them, panting.

With the muleta, Rodríguez takes risks, the bull almost catching him several times, while the plaza seems to contract around him and his work. Then, while he attempts a chest-high pass—a *pase de pecho*—to the right, his feet catch against each other, delay his retreat for just too long. And, directly in front of me, perhaps thirty yards away, I see a man's body jerked and hoisted into the air, shaken and bounced above a massive, implacably animal head while his limbs flap and turn against his will. His noiseless cry looks like a smile.

This perhaps takes two or three seconds while a few thin, female screams mix with a single punch of breath from all sides of the plaza. I watch through the telephoto lens of my camera and I take photographs and keep taking photographs until my film runs out.

Then the man is on the ground, flattening himself to the sand as the bull nuzzles in hugely, tries to lift him again and the peones leap forward, self-forgetting, caping the animal off and to the right. They pick Rodgríguez up and he is cradled, sitting upright, between two men, who carry him off to the Infirmary Gate in what seems a terribly primitive, damaging, joltingly human embrace. His face is set, ashen, while, below the waist, he is entirely soaked in his own blood, his talleguilla a solid, slick crimson.

The crowd applaud him as he leaves. They know they may be giving an ovation to a dying man and, in the corrida logic, this is no intrusion, this is a respectful farewell. Because his blood is an, albeit unwanted, part of the spectacle, because his head is still high, because he is bearing his pain well with only a tremble at the jaw and dulling eyes. He is playing his part.

And should I have photographed him, because he was bleeding for me to see, because to waste this insanity would be to make it even less eloquent, to make his best efforts pass without trace? Or should I have let him be, while my hands began to sweat against the camera casing and I used its magnifying eye to help me pay too much attention, to try to know, to understand? I turn to the woman beside me and, as I expected, she looks at me as if I were a slightly alien thing, the shutter release having given me away.

But, of course, nothing is over yet. López must come out and finish Rodríguez' task. He goes quickly for the kill, placing the sword poorly. The bull, its horns thick with human blood, its pelt thick with its own, stands. The peones perform the *rueda de peones*, swaying their capes at either side of the bull to make it shift its head from left to right and hopefully work the sword through an artery as it moves. This has no effect and, for a moment, the toreros simply stare at a bloody, dismally tenacious bull. They might almost be boys, mystified by some large matter they have set in motion, but lack the power to finish or control. Finally, the descabello comes and the bull sinks.

López now fights his own bull with a new coolness, a new level of commitment. Although it seems skittish and leery of any encounters with cape or horse, he coaxes it into a kind of calm. Suddenly, the floodlights kick in and, for the first time, I can see why the traje is the Suit of Lights—López sparkles, shines, his movements become smoother, more assured. Working with the muleta, he threads the bull under each arm, slips it in next to his stomach and chest. *Olés* start from the plaza, any thoughts of Rodríguez' pain apparently forgotten as López works. Still, the kill is difficult, the extinguishing of so much life a troublesome thing. The estocada is again followed, after a bloody pause, by the descabello.

But the audience is happy, is anxious to be positive now, to have a celebration, and López is granted a lap of honour. After the stresses of the day, he finally seems to grow to his full height, to truly *be* a killer of bulls, walking carefully, elegantly around the circle of sand as fans, hats, flowers, are thrown for him. His banderillero stoops on his behalf, gathers the flowers, passes on the items to be graced with a matador's touch and then tossed back to their owners. Another skill for the matador to learn: how to spin smoothly inside applause, how to throw a fan back to its owner gracefully, without it opening, how to best display the glow of survival, glistening brighter than the traje on his skin.

Unhappy Contreras, the leg of his traje taped shut, has to follow this triumph. He tries to win over the crowd by dedicating the bull to it, but then plays the animal poorly, pushes it beyond its endurance in an attempt to excel. His kill, when it comes, is greeted with moderate approval.

I leave the plaza, surrounded by companionably chatting crowds, murmurs of concern for Rodríguez occasionally breaking through. Outside, I pick my way through the little stalls selling fake banderillas and posters, toy bulls, soft drinks, bags of nuts. The sun is setting with low streaks and slashes of violent, yellow light and the air is growing unmistakably chill.

And I feel I have learned very little. Although I have been warned that the aficionado might expect a truly great corrida only once in every twenty years, I still wasn't expecting this. The corrida, it seems, can only reveal what beauties it might have if the observer is willing to ignore a great deal of clumsiness, ugliness and confusion, a great many failures of good faith and technique. The spectacle appears to be photogenic, but not filmic—to show best in frozen moments of poise, set aside from the vagaries of the bull, the slips and fumbles of the man, the interludes and distractions which continually break the kind of sustained artistry described in tales of the matador greats like Antonio Ordóñez whose artistry with the capote would have been hypnotising, even without the bull, whose contact with duende became mythical.

Or were those contacts simply myths? I've watched Ordóñez on film, albeit in twitchy black and white, and he didn't move me. Episodic and atmospheric, laden with a wealth of history, symbolism and the presence of death, perhaps the corrida is only fully alive for the story-teller, in the written word. It does, after all, provide the author with rich meat and flowers when the pen can ease over imperfections, direct the reader's focus to the points of importance and emotion, weave a screen across the plaza through which only beauty is visible.

I can, of course, hardly expect to draw sweeping conclusions from one corrida with novillero matadors. But I have to record that I do not understand how the corrida I saw today could be worth any living thing's injury or death. And yet it did involve the slaughter of six bulls and the severe wounding of one man. I do not understand how the aficionado's passion for toreo can tolerate the shambles which is a bad corrida. Which brings me again to matters beyond common sense, to questions of love and faith—both shot through with spilled blood.

The following morning I buy the papers in Madrid airport and read—in the Culture section—of the "Bloody Las Ventas Debut" of Otto Rodríguez, see the photographs of his body caught, cartwheeling on the bull's horns. Along with a review of each novillero's performance, there is the customary, detailed description of Rodríguez' injuries, quoted from the plaza infirmary's chief surgeon. It lists three cornadas, all high on the inner thighs, each wound fifteen centimetres long, one touching his femoral artery. His condition is officially pronounced *grave*—serious, but not dangerous. Wounds are categorised as *leve, menos grave, grave* and—the most serious—*más grave*.

The tossing action of the bull's head and the curve of its horns mean that cornadas are often multiple and, within each wound, there may be more than one twisting path of penetration to be opened, cleaned and then sutured. Specialist taurine surgeons can repair these injuries remarkably well, but the severing of the femoral artery and the immediate catastrophic blood loss resulting can defeat even the finest doctors. My Grandfather, once the safety man in his factory, told me all about the vulnerabilities of the femoral artery: the way the spray from it could paint a wall in moments. It is hardly surprising that all first-class plazas have fully equipped and staffed operating theatres standing ready, next to the ring. And Otto Rodríguez was lucky, he will survive, will be able, in due course, to advertise his first appearance at Las Ventas as having been dignified by the shedding of blood.

Some aficionados like to believe that horns themselves have healing properties. The fact that these insanitary projectiles bring with them (at the very least) blood, sand, grit and fragments of traje when they penetrate the torero makes this more than unlikely. But perhaps it is easier to watch a goring if you can believe a little something about the horn is kind.

I sit in the café, drinking water and taking another pill to get me through the journey, through the lifting, through the cramped grip of the aeroplane seats. And I seem no closer to understanding anything about the corrida than when I began. A video loop takes me through a two-hour delay, extolling the joys of coffee, over and over again, when even the thought of caffeine makes me twitch. And this trip seems to have gone the way my life goes: the first influx of fugitive information, the patterns of contact coming clear, the heat of a broken touch, incomprehension.

I have to see more corridas.

Chapter Seven

The Gate of Fear

Fear and pain can open a way to bring in their own duende, a kind of acute peace beyond the unendurable and before the next nasty surprise. Thus, absolute terror can occasionally break to reveal apparent courage, nerveless poise. I have occasionally met people in whom some unreasonable exposure to horror, destruction, loss has produced a deep-seated calm, a permanently altered sense of priorities. These individuals can often have about them a certain joy, not unlike a delight more usually seen in children—an ability to be pleased by things, in and of themselves, because of a freedom from distraction. For children this may come from an unencumbered, unexplored life. In adults it can be encouraged by the knowledge that much of the detail of life can be burned through to nothing in less than a breath. So too much innocence and too much experience can bring about the same effects.

I mention this by way of an introduction to the first matador whose work I found beautiful, Domingo López Ortega who used the nom de guerre "Domingo Ortega." Film exists of one of his appearances in Las Ventas,

Madrid, in 1956 and so I have seen him, seated in the audience at a testimonial corrida for the long-legged and, by that date, long-retired matador Nicanor Villalta.

Because this is not a conventional corrida, but a *festival*, those participating wear only the *traje corto*—the stylishly plain vaquero costume—as they duly turn, bewilder and kill their bulls. And then the audience calls for "Domingo Ortega," a matador two years into his own retirement—they want to see him play a bull.

A noticeably slim man in a light, single-breasted suit, collar and tie, he steps into the ring, hair slightly awry, smile quiet. He might be a doctor or a teacher—some distant, monochrome relative, called on to deliver a party piece. But then he begins with the bull and becomes himself.

With the bull, Ortega's movements slip between formality, elegance and play, there is always a great deal of play, of physically evident delight. Face calm, ready, somehow, to be pleasantly surprised, he checks and curves the path of the skinny, young animal with the capote and sets it capering about him. The dominance of the man is so absolute that it appears loving, paternal. There can be no danger here, because Ortega will admit none.

During the faena he bows, swoops and pirouettes, each action drawing the bull in closer. From time to time Ortega strokes its horn while it passes, looking at him, or smoothes at its side with his palm when it passes to turn for him again. Immensely flexible, but controlled, he leads the bull low to left and right, or lifts its head as he wishes, as they both appear to wish. He performs a *molinete* and then another, swirling the muleta out around him as he turns in something which is more than an *adorno*—a cheap trick involving no danger—something which is a celebration of this moment, these creatures, this breath, this fine time they are having together. Man and animal, animal and man, they might have known each other all their lives. Watching them, it seems quite possible that this integrated motion might simply continue, that there is no reason for it to ever stop. Even after the sword has gone in clean to the hilt and Ortega has stepped away, the bull skips after him, seems unaware it's over now.

Ortega, the veteran of so many plazas, the man who faced Belmonte's "deep" toreo and took it deeper, closer still—he could bring calm to the ring, an absence of fear, a joy. I am reminded, when I see him, of the way Monty Roberts* works with unbroken horses, taking them to an understanding of themselves and men. The impossibility of what Roberts does, the crossing of the species barrier, the palpable gentleness, is immensely moving. He has decades of experience in "breaking" horses his way, the way that doesn't involve breaking, and often demonstrates his skills in front of audiences. By now he is used to ringside observers weeping, even fainting when they see two completely different creatures communicate, when they see a change achieved in a potentially deadly animal without cruelty, feel an injustice of their own touched by the possibility of something that should have been better, different. The ones who faint were usually abused as children. Roberts can understand this: he was, too.

*C.f., *The Man Who Listened to Horses*.

But Roberts doesn't end his interaction with the horse by, for example, shooting it. Aficionados will entirely disagree, but perhaps the division of energies at the heart of the corrida is not between the intentions and skills of the man and the brute force and dangerous unpredictability of the bull. Perhaps the contradiction comes when the moment of animal meeting is hampered by injury and followed by the kill. Although, naturally, if the bull is a beef-providing animal, it will be killed—that is the truth of the Moment of Truth. Would it be dishonest, dishonourable, to play the bull and then kill it cleanly elsewhere? Would this begin to turn a ritual into a circus act? Is the art of the corrida in the close physical relation of two moving forms, or in the threat of death, or can't the two be separated?

And even Roberts, of course, doesn't leave his horses unscathed. He removes them from the wild state for ever and fits them for a life spent in service. He takes them through what David Attenborough calls "the barriers that mankind, for the past 30,000 years or so, has been building between himself and the natural world." Speaking of his meeting with potentially deadly wild gorillas, he says, "I was overcome with a surge of joy . . . During those few minutes those barriers had been annihilated and we had experienced a unity and a harmony which for most of our lives in our man-made world, we can glimpse only dimly. In my belief, it is that harmony which, in the end, must underlie all true happiness."*

*"The Happiness Lectures," Radio 4, 3 July 1999.

Fear has been removed by tenderness, replaced by wonder.

As I have mentioned before, mankind produces different loves—among them the one that seeks to preserve its love untouched, the one that seeks to break it and the one that worships with the kill.

Domingo López Ortega had a love of the last kind for bulls. Born poor to a family of farm labourers, he grew up in cattle country. He learned the matador's craft as best he could in capeas and novillados and in 1928, aged just twenty, his performance as an espontáneo was so good that he made his debut in the full traje the next day. The following year he took his alternativa and was instantly hailed as a maestro. He redefined toreo. He faced the bull three-quarters-on, actually stepped into its path and used the flexibility his stance gained him to increase his interaction with the animal. With low, slow passes, he increased the curve of the bull's course around his body, and his exposure to its horns, bringing the extent of the close turns to a full 180 degrees. This created an entirely new, intense relationship between the animal and the man, a "deep" toreo. Perhaps unsurprisingly, he was seriously wounded several times, but made it to retirement in 1954. As I have mentioned, it was Ortega who was accused of letting the side down by bringing the widespread incidence of horn-shaving to the attention of the press in 1952.* As I have mentioned, someone

---

*In this he stood shoulder-to-shoulder with matador Antonio Benvenida, his friend.

who has experienced great pain and fear may develop an altered sense of priorities.

In the spring of 1999 I went to Seville to see more corridas in the Feria de Abril. Among a number of other matadors, I would watch "El Juli,"* the seventeen-year-old, apparently entirely fearless, rising star, and Curro Romero, now at least sixty-five, one of the most shamefully timid toreros in the corrida's history. I would also watch Enrique Ponce, a man who took his alternativa in the year I completed my first book, an alternativa which, tracing back four generations of senior matadors, was passed from the hands of Domingo Ortega.

Take it for granted that Seville in the feria is a sun-aching, glorious place and that even the rather dismal airport has its clusters of girls in flamenco dresses and outbursts of laughter. Also that the old town is splendid with narrow, Moorish streets and photogenic squares, horse-drawn carriages, leather goods, peculiarly annoying ceramics and a general air of tapas-nibbling bonhomie and sleek content. Also that the gypsies and beggars have considerable dignity. Also that the pre-Christian Giralda tower is bathed in spotlights throughout the night and, therefore, surrounded by tourists, disorientated pigeons and bats. I liked to stand under the tower at night.

Take it for granted that lifting and travelling still hurt

---

*"El Juli" recently appeared in an advertisement which showed him emerging from the plaza and eyeing a new car—at which point he was reminded that he's still too young to drive.

my neck, that nothing much is different or even interesting with me.

But I, nevertheless, arrive and compose myself and make my way carefully through a languid evening, down towards the Maestranza bull ring—a glowing, curved confection of white walls, tawny sand and ox-blood paint. Outside the plaza, a massive crowd is meandering across all four lanes of the nearest road: people chatting, smoking, flirting, ambling home. The sun sets, hot in feathers of cloud.

I walk a few side streets further, the pain in my spine not too strident, and find—as I was told to—a bar run by a former matador called Franco Cardeño. I've read my Hemingway—this is a bullfighting book, there has to be at least one bar, at least one bar story, even if I listened to it sober, while drinking my own weight in water and eating ham.

This particular bar, the Bodegón Portagayola, is tiny but, like many aficionado bars, is still well supplied with old corrida posters, stuffed toro de lidia heads and mounted ears. The ears look a little like hairy children's shoes while the heads are truly, quite simply monstrous, even as glassy-eyed still lifes. And one has a more than average significance—it's the bull which battered away half the face of Franco Cardeño.

Cardeño, as part of a cartel organised for older (and, frankly, never-completely-made-it) matadors, appeared in La Maestranza and decided to try his hand, taking the bull a porta goyola. Sadly, I was told, he lost his nerve as he knelt, waiting, and began to stand just as the bull charged towards him out of the toril. Franco also man-

aged to then hold his cape in front of his face. Not a recommended thing to do.

The result of this sad combination of events gives
the Bodegón Portagayola its name and much of its
taurine display: a photograph of Franco on the sand
and bleeding, Franco in hospital with his cheek taped
back in place, the head of the bull to blame staring
out from the wall and across at Franco as he works at
the bar, cutting ham with an impressively long knife.
Sr. Cardeño is also, of course, his own memorial, with
his lifelessly concave right cheek below a vaguely dis-
tracted eye. And, as my guide for the evening points
out, Franco currently has a bandaged thumb—accident
with the ham slicing. Welcome to Andalucia, home of
the toro bravo. Welcome to a town obsessed with the
corrida.

And welcome to La Maestranza. Late afternoon on
22nd April, and I walk down to the plaza. I could close
my eyes and find my way here, just by the smell: expensive perfume, hair oil, sweet aftershave, Romeo y Julieta
cigars. The tangle of little streets, cafés, bars begins to
thicken with people a few blocks above La Maestranza.
And many of them are Beautiful People and many know
it. One man stands, foot lifted on the shoe-shiner's
block, head high, spine frighteningly straight, hair
immaculately glossy, shirt fresh from the laundry, linen
suit creaseless, spotless, quite lacking in any contact with
reality. His unshined shoe is just as brilliant as the
shined one, but he has it brushed again, in any case,
while he smokes his cigar, looks about him, eyes neu-

trally Ray-Banned but still suggesting something like contempt.

Because Julián López López—"El Juli"—is appearing today, there is a dense crowd waiting near Gate 16, the torero's entrance. Young girls, sticky with hormones, clutch photographs for the teenage maestro to sign, and the usual respectful/curious craning to see the cuadrillas enter has an uncharacteristically pressing edge. Someone calls, "It's time," and the first line of shining men, men dressed for another world, files quietly through, concentration all elsewhere. "El Juli" isn't here yet, the crowd can wait.

Son of a failed novillero, "El Juli" burst on the scene as a full matador last year. When I was in Madrid, his name was everywhere—a home boy, trained in the Madrid school, making good, making very good. He'd just been carried in triumph out of Las Ventas' principal gate after a masterful confirmation of his alternativa. He was interviewed in his parents' middle-class living room: a clean-cut schoolboy with a matador's signature curving facial scar: far less anxious to talk about himself than his father. After facing bulls in South America while he was too young to work in Europe, "El Juli" distinguished himself in Spain and France—possibly while he was still under age.

By the end of last year's Spanish season "El Juli" had cut close to 150 ears. He went on to excel in South American corridas, weathered an injury there, and is now back in Spain. He's seventeen, has been dubbed "the Mozart of Toreo" and is electrifying the corrida. He is often teamed with Enrique Ponce, who is married to his apoderado's daughter, making them the corrida equivalent of brothers-in-law, I suppose. "El Juli" continues to explore his seemingly endless ability to change styles and entrance audiences. Ponce, meanwhile, is an established maestro, a Valencian, now twenty-eight, who has stayed at or near the top rank of his profession since 1992. His frequent pairing with "El Juli" seems to be allowing him to rediscover his craft, to push what he's learned, what he's felt through all his years in the ring, just a little further. Together, they are making people talk of a new Golden Age.

The first bull "El Juli" tackles today is manso. It doesn't like to run, preferring to pause and sniff the air, dipping its head to the sand in a memory of grazing. What little vigour it has collapses after the picadors have done their work. It's very obvious that the public expects a great deal of "El Juli," the plaza is gently restless with need, but he has a hard time making the bull move through groups of passes—*tandas*. The animal is dangerous now, conserving its strength and making savage flicks of its head as "El Juli" moves in.

At the kill, the young man's sword hits bone, again and again and again while the silence presses down against him. He tries for the descabello. Five blows later and the animal finally falls. This is hardly a good beginning, but "El Juli" bears it well, walks back to the barrera with carefully presented dignity.

And, when its time comes, his next bull is slightly better and he seems determined to make what he can of it. His almost girlish face seems placid, almost oblivious, as he makes his approaches with the capote, performs a graceful *gaonera*—a move where the matador holds the cape behind him, draws the bull, then turns and draws it again. He performs *chicuelinas*, citing the bull from the front, then turning close towards it as it comes and folding the cape back around himself, ready to draw the bull again from the opposite side. He purses his lips during each tanda, licks them when he's concluded. Wearing the montera, he seems especially young, as if he were in some peculiar school uniform.

After the banderillas, which seem to disturb the animal enormously, "El Juli" sets to work; shrugging his shoulders back, leading with his crotch, he fits his body into the customary bow-curve of the matador, curling his toes as he steps into the move that will trigger the bull to follow. Very quickly, his traje is coated with blood from brushing contacts with the animal. A mobile phone goes off and is tutted and shushed by most of the audience. "El Juli" calls to the bull, as all matadors do, but his high, boyish voice seems incongruous while he does a man's work. The bull is staggering, almost drowning with fatigue, but "El Juli" stays with it, trying to lift it. At the last, with a visible exertion of will, he produces a surge of movement, a series of electrifying passes which leave the plaza saying "Sssssi!" He loses the muleta as he goes for the kill, but slips in the sword in one movement. This time he is granted a lap of honour which he takes with a light, quietly dutiful air. When he leaves the ring, his father claps him on the ear in congratulation—he's been a good boy. He ignores the gesture. This hasn't been a great day, not by his usual standards.

Twenty-four hours later and I'm back in the plaza. I have to cross the entrance of the toril to reach my seat and find the air caught in that sandy, ominous corridor is unmistakably charged. As usual, latecomers in this arena without aisles have to scramble up the tendidos, relying on the kindness of strangers to let them through. It amuses me to watch the rich and impeccable wrestle slowly into place, alongside the parties of housewives, the working-class fathers, carefully introducing the corrida to their sons. I can state from experience that squeezing through to a distant seat can give anyone you pass more than ample opportunity to run their hands, gently but unmistakably, over pretty much anything they'd like. The heat is astonishing, the press of flesh on every side unmistakably adhesive.

And "El Juli" is back, too, this time on the same cartel as Ponce and with the King's mother watching from the President's box. The bulls are from the Jandilla ganadería (yesterday's were from María del Carmen Camacho) but they seem equally dispirited and unhappy with their lot. Most like hovering near the toril door, taking up a *querencia* there—a favourite spot the bull will always seek to return to for private reasons of its own—perhaps the sand is cool there, or carries an interesting scent—and where a matador cannot enter without extreme risk to himself. A querencia can be employed to make a bull charge, if the matador blocks its return to its place of safety.

I have already watched Curro Romero refuse to have almost anything to do with his bull, never mind its horns. He has killed his first with a blade placed so poorly that its tip protruded from the bull's flank, pearling gore. As the animal coughed up blood, staring, bemused, at each new flux, the peones tried a rueda de peones to make the blade move in the bull's body and sever anything, anything at all that might be quickly fatal, but in the end the bull was finally, messily finished after three descabellos. A few days before, Romero had given one of his rare, transcendent performances, for the sake of his new love, but not today. Now the crowd wants something better, much better than a mix of quite understandable, but inadvertently cruel, cowardice.

And, when I see "El Juli" through my binoculars, I know he has decided to be better, the very best. The whole cast of his face has altered, it seems almost middle-aged, and his movements have a new weight, a new significance. Today he is going to make something happen—the force of will he showed in flickers yesterday is naked now and irrevocably locked.

His bull is weak through the capote work, tumbles head over heels as its legs give way, but "El Juli" is with it, he's on song. Once the faena has worked into its flow, the President gives the signal and a paso doble strikes up; "El Juli," padding in under its rhythm, laces passes together and raises "*Olés*" with almost each shift of his wrist. When the bull barges him, he simply lets himself spin back, whirls the cape, improvises a molinete between its horns. This is unheard of, almost mystifying, even for the knowledgeable Seville audience. He kills with conviction, although he has to go in twice, and is awarded an ear. Once again he steps around the ring to receive his ovation, accepting flowers and tokens, touching and returning fans, hats, a jacket and a waistcoat.

This first success leaves the audience with hopes for more and, with "Ostrero," his second bull, "El Juli" seems coolly determined to give them what they want. He selects a pair of the matador's customary white banderillas to cheers of approval. With this toro, he will place his own banderillas. The cheers fade when he chooses to begin by standing on the estribo to strike in the first pair. The plaza only relaxes a touch when the bull refuses to charge the man where he perches, almost completely trapped, inviting a cornada. Now "El Juli" places the three pairs of "sticks," running across the sand, efficient and neat—Ponce watchful and fatherly behind the barrera. The crowd's mood has changed now, tightened, edged towards something unpredictable—"El Juli" is working the plaza just as much as the bull, and there seems to be no way of knowing where the afternoon will take us. Having asked to see the edge of possibility, aficionados now find themselves peering over it. All six banderillas are placed in silence and then hailed with an explosion of relieved delight.

The toro is slow in the faena, it stalls in the midst of charges and hooks its head. Time and again it seems that "El Juli" will be caught, but still he nudges closer and closer to the bull with successions of faultlessly linked tandas, threading in left-handed *naturales* and chest passes which prepare the bull for its final lunge. Now and again there are cries of astonishment, hisses of alarmed breath, but otherwise the plaza is silent.

And then it comes, the reality behind the fear of injury, the fear that "El Juli" himself seems to lack. One last time, the bull halts and won't take the lure. The matador stands his ground, insanely close to the animal's head and, quicker than I could have imagined, the charge punches forward, "El Juli" is caught, lifted up between the bull's horns, bounced over its back and dropped to the sand. Ponce is quick across the sand to be with his friend, to lift him up. The peones cape away the danger and Ponce begins leading "El Juli" away towards the enfermería, but the young man shakes his protector off, speaks to him* and then I watch Ponce clear the banderilleros away. "El Juli," limping now, unsteady, is going to make the kill, to finish the job. There is blood where his talleguilla gapes on his left thigh, his own blood.

"El Juli" faces the bull and kills it in one full stroke. There was never a thought he'd do anything else. For this instant, his certainty holds the ring, we are inside it, his moment, his eye in the storm. The bull sways, the man sways. And then the animal drops, perhaps a second later "El Juli" subsides into the arms of two peones.

Then, as the cheers rise, Julián López López is lifted up and the Maestranza begins to chant "To-re-ro! To-re-ro! To-re-ro!," something unheard of in this most urbane and cool-eyed plaza. The man's journey to the infirmary gate is treated as a triumph—as indeed it is. He has just become the first matador to be carried out through the infirmary gate, in lieu of the Puerta del Príncipe. One of his banderilleros accepts his ovation in his place.

Tonight, the corrida over, the crowd doesn't drift away. At the front of the Maestranza, an ambulance is parked, motor running, close to the infirmary door. Inside, aficionados wait by the infirmary notice board

---

*Allegedly "El Juli" said to Ponce, "If you want to help me, get them [the cuadrilla] out of here. I have a bull to kill."

for the official posting of "El Juli's" injuries. Outside, people are gathered around the ambulance, look down at it from the balcony, stand on the wall by the railings to see more of the "Nothing yet" which is happening. There are mumbles of concern, scatters of conversation praising the day's toreo and then faltering into silence— he didn't look badly injured, but you never can tell.

Then the stretcher emerges, the crowd gives an inquisitive nudge forward, press and amateur cameras flash. A plump, serious boy, sitting up on his father's shoulders, is just able to reach out and touch the ambulance window. He is, perhaps, eight or nine with his hair in a crew cut. When he turns his head, I can see that he has a coleta, the matador's pigtail of fine hair, left long at the nape of the neck.

In the morning, every news stand is draped in headlines trumpeting "El Juli" and his bloody success, and shows pictures of his body, suspended above the horns of toro number 31, "Ostrero." His wound is reported as a minor—*menos grave*—cornada to the muscle in his left thigh.* At the Maestranza, the blood-caked banderillas he used yesterday are quietly on sale for anyone who could bear to buy that much good or bad luck. In *El País*, Joaquín Vidal calls "El Juli" a "Vulcan of bravery and corrida mastery." So the public's love affair continues, spreading beyond strictly taurine circles—even reaching the British press—alarming those who wish to keep children away from the corrida, and delighting

---

*Later that week the diminutive matador Domingo Valderrama would face a Miura bull and take a *más grave* cornada in an almost identical place. Although surgeons managed to save his leg, it is very unlikely that he will fight seriously again.

television companies, aficionados and plaza managers alike.

Not that Spain hasn't loved this way before. "Manolete"—Manuel Laureano Rodríguez Sánchez y Sánchez—was, one could say, the aficionado's Diana Spencer. The man General Franco liked to have his picture taken alongside. The son of a prostitute and a matador from Cordoba, he made his debut at twelve, in 1929, and—the confusions of the Civil War and his duties as an artillery man intervening—he took his alternativa in 1939. A sad-eyed, long-faced matador with a complicated love-life, he was called "the Knight of the sorrowful countenance" and was both worshipped and vilified in the press. His style of toreo was adjudged "safe" because he sited the bull in profile, but proved dangerous—and popular—because he still brought the bull close to his body, close enough for him to suffer serious cornadas.

By August 1947, when Manolete faced Islero, the bull that killed him, he was on or over the brink of a nervous breakdown and drinking heavily. The cornada he received severed his femoral artery and he died at 5:06 the following morning. His death was followed by a predictably hysterical outpouring of guilty mourning, the press and aficionados managing to be both self-righteous and self-flagellating as they blamed each other for the massive pressures under which he was expected to perform the corrida's equivalent of miracles.

Those pressures, of course, were not unique to Manolete. A matador like "El Juli" or Enrique Ponce faces a barrage of media attention. Beyond that, there is the price for realising a vocation, the tension between the dream and the fact, the depth of emotional injury that may become just as likely as delight. And with the matador's vocation, of course, there is the matter of physical injury, of death—the extension of your future's threats to touch anyone who touches you. Ponce's wife and parents never watch his corridas. They wait for him together, shut away from all news, until he comes back to them, tells them what happened carefully, makes it safe. After that, they can bear to watch his work, replayed on film. As senior matador in corridas he is quietly, presciently vigilant, ready to co-ordinate protection for the fallen, often the first on hand. In private life, he keeps his family as protected as he can.

And, in the ring, he is outstanding. I saw him perform twice in Seville, once with "El Juli" and then, the following day, on the same cartel as the two Madrileños, Miguel Baéz Spinola—"Litri"—and Manuel Díaz González—"El Cordobes."

In the first corrida, Ponce's first bull was dispirited and weak. A toss of the animal's horns took the capote from the man's hands, but Ponce nodded, innocent-eyed, as if to say, "It's okay, you can take that." Then he picked up the rhythm again, trying to build something from nothing before the picadors moved in.

As "El Juli" performed the *quite* between pics, as the banderillas were placed, at every shift and turn of the bull, Ponce was utterly focused, decoding, unlocking the movements of the toro, preparing what would have to be done, letting it sink below intellect into instinct. And then he walked into the faena, quietly, softly attempted to move the bull away from its own mind and to shape it according to his. But the toro was panting, exhausted, over-weakened by the pics. Ponce talked to it, called to it, tilting his head, easing them both through moves, and then, as the bull staggered to a final stand-still, went for the sword.

The bull coughed blood, sometimes a sign that the matador has faked the kill and gone into the side, avoid-ing the horn. In this case, the kill was honourable, but the blood was disapproved of anyway. No ear would be cut this time, no lap of honour granted. Ponce watched the death until the bull was down and gone, looked dis-contented as he walked away. There is no matador he competes with more fiercely than himself.

The second bull was just as bad, Ponce's eyes lifting heavenward as he tried to do his job, but always his focus was on the bull, almost visibly on the bull. The line of his attention stretched, entirely unbroken, from the moment the animal entered the ring to the moment he took its life.

The next day, opinion in the plaza is divided: will Ponce be unsettled by the injury of his friend, dispirited by a feria which has provided a succession of poor bulls? Or will he show the character that has made him, and kept him, Spain's leading matador for so long? Will he use the pressure to lift himself beyond himself?

I have spent my morning visiting the Virgin of the Macarena—the matador's Virgin. Enthroned at the heart of her church, she is plump-faced and straight-backed, carefully dressed in embroidered robes, stiff as a traje. Fat, embossed tears cling to her cheeks like blue birthmarks and she looks either slightly sad, or slightly stern, depending on how close I stand to her. Presumably, she has been captured in the act of weeping for toreros.

But now I am in La Maestranza again, waiting for my last corrida. Vendors pick their ways through us calling out, *"Cerveza, coka, agua,"* or trying to sell nuts, or paper sun shades. The usual waves of cigar smoke and ash are starting to roll with the breeze. Below me are two young men, impeccably dressed in black *trajes cortos* with crimson carnation buttonholes. Although the temperature is in the nineties, neither has broken a sweat. As usual, my notebook, my two cameras and my binoculars amuse the aficionados around me. When I say that I'm from Scotland they smile at me as if I'm joking or harmlessly mad. I smile back, I would hope sanely, and try to settle into another two hours or so of sitting upright, of trying to make my neck muscles relax, of thinking the pain away.

Down in the callejón, the paseíllo over, Ponce is walking, dark eyes slightly surprised—*here I am again*. He moves calmly, pats shoulders, embraces, his gaze constantly drawn to the open, waiting sand. Out in the unwatered ring, dust rises.

Ponce's first bull is far less fit than anything I've seen before, confused, weak and tremulous. It is almost immediately rejected. A herd of massive, prehistoric-looking steers, high-horned red and white creatures with ludicrous bells around their necks, are driven, clanging and lowing, into the ring, in the hope that the bull will take to them and leave when they are driven out again. This is the theory—I have read about it repeatedly. Ten minutes, and much clanging, later the bull is finally lured out by the flicker of capes waved at it over the barrera. Ponce looks on with disgust.

But, before the next bull is brought, the matador calms himself, stepping onto the sand and sweeping out with the capote, meditative, creating the space he needs to work. The animal isn't exactly promising, but the man takes it, catches it in a rhythm, swinging it close around him, scooping it up behind media veronicas that lash out from his waist. Ponce talks to the toro gently, slightly impatiently, as he might to a large, drunk friend.

The faena lasts six minutes: six minutes of coaxing and pauses, of flowing tandas which see Ponce citing to left and right, slipping to one knee and up again. The dust lifts about the pair as they tighten on each other. Sweat rolls off Ponce's face. As the paso doble plays, he arches his body high and back, paces, becomes the only man I have seen to fully inhabit the shape of a matador, to take and overwhelm the required positions as if they were his choice, his invention. And all this serving one focus, the bull, the animal on which he is utterly intent.

He has risked a long faena, working on the bull, steadying it, but still the kill goes badly and a time warning* sounds as Ponce tries to finish the job and the regulation twelve minutes for the kill expire. Three times he goes in with the sword, then there is a rueda de

---

*If a matador takes more than the regulation twelve minutes to kill the bull, a warning trumpet—*aviso*—will be sounded. After a further five minutes, another *aviso* will be given and, after a further three minutes, the bull will be taken from the matador and led out by the plaza's herd of steers.

peones, then three descabellos before the animal sways and falls.

As the bull sinks, Ponce faces it, head craned forward, right arm thrown wide, the other cradling the muleta while he appears to think the animal to death. Most matadors face the bull as it dies, but I have never seen the gesture filled with this tension, this sense of worship and violation, this naked hunger for a soul. There is something about watching Ponce which brings on the sensation of watching the impossible.

Making his way back to the barrera, he appears to be deeply drained.

One rejected and two seriously inadequate bulls later, Ponce's next toro enters the ring, halting almost as soon as it touches the sand and looking up at the audience, amazed. Next, it gallops towards the nearest burladero and knocks a huge splinter of wood from it with one swipe. Peones, seeking to help a nervous matador with a truco, will sometimes cape a bull into the burladero, whipping the cloth away at the last minute to leave the animal headbutting solid wood and possibly giving itself concussion. This can be highly counter-productive—a concussed bull is extremely unpredictable. Today's toro simply looks deeply uneasy and very keen to stay in a querencia near the toril gate.

Ponce starts as he means to go on, movements liquid and assured, talking to the toro, sometimes almost seeming to strike a bargain as he winds it in around him. When he wants it to stand at the end of a tanda, it stands, fixed with a firm remate, when he wants it to follow his hands, it follows.

Standing in the *medios*, the central area of the ring, Ponce removes his hat and slowly turns, holding it up for us. This will be our bull, he is giving us this death. He throws the montera and it lands upside-down, open, but then flips. There is an audible relief in the plaza as it indulges its superstitions—now the montera can't fill with the matador's blood. A few swallows dip down, skreeling, into the plaza, lithe in the heat, on the hunt.

The faena picks up his conversation with the bull as if the pair had never missed a beat. Ponce takes the bull away from its injury, its distress, dances it towards its death. And I understand why, beneath the banal sexuality of the skin-tight silk, there is something sexual about the faena. When the paso doble kicks in again, when Ponce lets his arms open, tosses back his head and simply walks with enough presence to touch 14,000 people, he brings himself into a space he has created where one living creature seems to entirely anticipate the physical will of another.

To human eyes, this preparation for a death can look like a place of safety, a place where our needs are unfolded for us, where we can transcend ourselves, not alone. Matadors often liken the faena to making love. Like "Domingo Ortega," Ponce has moved beyond simple dominance. The matador appears to clear a way through the air with his muleta for exactly the path the bull desires to follow. Rather than tricking the bull, Ponce gives the impression that he knows what it wants before it does, that he is here to help. This is the body knowledge of a lover, played out as theatre and execution.

Every time the bull falters or stalls, Ponce stays with it, closer and closer, the animal's blood slowly painting the front of his traje, no one in the world but them, no one in the world but us, because he has cited us, too, drawn us into the inexorable movement towards his goal, the kill.

Ponce fetches the sword, makes the last, loaded passes in faultless silence and then darts in. Something buckles in the air, blinks. And then there is applause while the bull sways and its legs fold under it. Ponce watches, arm extended, his whole body braced in the air, the faena not over until the last breath, until he takes the toro's life.

Which is as close as I've known the corrida get to a religious experience—the sight of man willing in, taking in, an animal's life. It is a strange thing to watch: an elaborately prepared transgression, a sacrifice and a sin, ugly and peculiarly moving.

Ponce takes his lap round the sand, an ear granted, a man who met his first bull in public when he was eleven, a man who undertakes over 100 corridas a year, a man who has made this his life, who has let this make its life in him. There are the customary courtesies and gifts. I feel myself wish him luck.

The following morning, early, I leave for home—not my favourite place. So, before I get there, one last story—about luck. About luck and Lorca's friend, Ignacio Sánchez Mejías.

Mejías was having money troubles and was forced back into the ring at forty-three, an unfit man and he knew it. People said he had the smell of death about him. He'd survived frequent, terrible gorings throughout his career, but even the most fortunate can find their luck runs out.

In Corunna, on 6 August 1934, Juan Belmonte, "Domingo Ortega" and Ignacio Sánchez Mejías were all on the same cartel. Belmonte went in for a kill, the sword hit bone, bent, sprang up and fell into the audience, killing a young spectator. Unlucky for him.

"Domingo Ortega" left for Madrid after the corrida, having just heard of the death of his brother. He crashed his car—unlucky for him—along the way and, shaken, asked Mejías if he would stand in for him on 11 August, at a corrida in Manzanares.

On the 11th, Mejías' car broke down and he had to travel by train, arriving late and walking straight into the sorteo selection at the hotel. He asked to fight first and, when he was refused the option, almost pulled out of the fight. Son of a doctor, overweight, old and filled with unease, he inspected the plaza infirmary and found it wanting. Unlucky for him, he insisted that he should be taken to Madrid—100 miles to the north over difficult roads—if he was gored.

And when Mejías faced "Granadino" he *was* gored. He had decided to prove his bravery, or banish his fear, by playing the bull while sitting on the estribo with his back hard against the barrera. This left him virtually immobilised and with a hard surface behind him, making sure that any horn which caught him would penetrate deeply. He made one successful high right-handed pass, the bull coming close enough to slit his talleguilla, but the bull turned and, as Mejías tried to stand, pierced him deeply in the right groin.

Mejías was, as he'd requested, prepared for the drive to Madrid with his wound cleaned and plugged, but the ambulance broke down for two hours along the way and finally reached the hospital a full thirteen hours after the cornada. By this time, gangrene had set in and Mejías lapsed into bouts of agonised seizures and hallucinations. He didn't die until 13 August.

Federico García Lorca—himself a Granadino—said that his friend had died taking part in a "religious mystery."

My journey home is uneventful. Inside the flat, I go through the usual routine: unpack, put in a load of washing, open the mail. By the end of the evening, I find myself in my study, the one where I used to write prose fiction. It's a room full of charms and statues, most of them intended to confer some sort of blessing, or at least a little luck. Among them is the figure from Granada, the cloaked and hooded man, stepping out above the word *Rescate*. Which, I was amused to find, translates as *Redemption*. Fancy buying that. And fancy it not making the journey from Granada to Glasgow intact. It broke, somewhere along the way. God tidying up my narrative again.

I sit down and try not to think that I've spent so many hours of my life here, working inside the space my work made for me, inside the vocation which has now closed with me outside. I don't know what to do.

Glossary

Acoso y derribo   Literally, "chase and knock down." A test at the *tienta* of the spirit of bulls destined for the ring. Now mainly out of use.

Adorno   Easy move in the ring involving no risk.

Afición   The quality of liking, having one's fancy taken by something. It can be used specifically to denote an informed, even opinionated, passionate interest in the *corrida*. To have it is to be an initiate in taurine circles, to be a believer.

Aficionado/a   Literally, someone who has a liking for anything, or who is a fan of anything. Quite often used specifically of those who have a knowledge of and enthusiasm for the *corrida*.

Afeitar   Horn-shaving.

Alguacil   A constable: the President's representative in the ring.

Alternativa   Matador's graduation ceremony.

Añadido   False *coleta*.

Aplombado   A bull that is leaden, low-headed, swollen-tongued and liable to chop with his horns.

Apoderado   Manager of a torero.

A porta goyola   See *larga cambiada de rodillas.*

Banderilla   The 27-inch dowel-stemmed dart, metal-tipped with a single barb, three pairs of which are intended to be thrown into the area around the bull's *morrillo* during the second phase of the corrida. The wooden stems are decorated with coloured paper strips. *Banderillas,* once placed, used to stand fairly proud of the bull's flesh, but have lately been made with a collapsible neck which makes them less of an obstruction to the *matador* as they now flop and rattle like surreal dreadlocks against the bull's haunches.

Banderillas de fuego   Gunpowder *banderillas.*

Banderillero   Placer of the *banderillas.* Also known as a *peon.*

Banderillero de confianza   Generally an older, experienced *torero* who acts as a kind of combined coach, caddy and psychotherapist to the *matador.*

Barrera   The wooden barrier which surrounds the bull ring.

Brindis   A toast which dedicates the death of a bull.

Burladeros   Four wooden screens placed around the ring that provide toreros with a refuge from the bull.

Cajón   Individual pen in which the bull is transported to the *corrida.*

Callejón The narrow passage between the *barrera* which surrounds the ring and the wall which fronts the first row of audience seating.

Capea An informal, illegal and often chaotic village square event, where sometimes bulls, sometimes cows and sometimes quite experienced and therefore dangerous animals are played by an occasionally massive crowd of amateurs.

Capote de brega The large cape the *matador* uses for his first passes with the bull.

Capote de paseo Lavishly embroidered parade cape.

Cargar la suerte See *suerte*.

Cartel The poster or bill used to advertise a *corrida*, or, more loosely, the list of *toreros* involved in a particular *corrida*, whose names would be shown on the *cartel*.

Casta The bull's fighting spirit.

Celoso Eager (of a bull).

Cerviguillo See *morrillo*.

Chaquetilla *Matador*'s jacket.

Charlotada "Comic" and often very grisly *corrida*. Not popular with *aficionados*, but the source of some passes now used in conventional corridas.

Chicuelina Pass invented by a comic *torero* introduced by "Chicuelo." The *matador* wraps the cape around himself as the bull passes.

Codicioso Hungry for action (of a bull).

Coleta Pigtail worn by all *toreros* (except the *picador*) as a mark of their profession.

Corbatín *Matador*'s narrow black tie.

Cornada The term for all but the most glancing penetration by a bull's horn.

Corrida de toros Literally means a running of the bulls. It is now the name attached specifically to a traditional Spanish "bullfight" carried out under current regulations, most usually with the killing of two bulls each by three fully fledged *matadors*. The bulls should weigh no less than 460 kg on the hoof and, in a first-category bull ring, should be between four and six years old.

Cuadrilla The team which supports the *matador* in the ring. This comprises two *picadors*, three *banderilleros* (known as *peones*), the *mozo de espada*, or sword boy, and his assistant.

Descabello A heavy, straight sword with a metal crosspiece near its tip.

Espada A blade, also a synonym for *matador*.

Espontáneo One who spontaneously (and illegally) jumps into the ring to show his prowess at *toreo*.

Estocada The killing sword (and the word for the stroke it makes).

Estoque de descabellar See *estocada*.

Estribo The wooden strip running round the *barrera*, to help *toreros* leap over it, if need be.

Faena   See *Suerte de Matar*.

Fijado   Literally, "fixed." Used in the *corrida* to describe the fixing of a bull's head close to the cape during passes.

Ganadería   Bull ranch.

Ganadero   Rancher who breeds bulls.

Gaonera   Pass where cape is held behind the back and the *matador* turns as the bull passes to "cite" again.

Larga cambiada de rodillas   A particularly dangerous pass involving kneeling before the gate from which the bull will issue. (Also known as an *a porta goyola*.)

Levantado   A bull that is unharmed, alert, easily tricked.

Machos   Tassels affixed at the edge of the *talleguilla* on the outside of the leg.

Mandar   To dominate and control the bull.

Manso   Cowardly (of a bull).

Matador   A killer of bulls, as opposed to a butcher, or murderer of bulls. Currently there are roughly 230 *matadors* in Spain. Like 90 per cent of Spanish breeders, agents and promoters, they are represented by the Confederation of Bullfighting Professionals.

Medios   Central area of the ring.

Molinete   Right-handed pass where both the man and the cape spin as the *toro* passes.

Monosabio   Literally, "wise monkey": a picador's aide.

Montera   *Matador*'s hat.

Morrillo   The highly developed head-tossing muscle in the bull's neck. In taurine circles *morillo* is almost always spelt with one r, but I am reliably informed—in as far as information can be reliable among those in love with controversy—that *morillo* means "firedog" and nothing else, while *morrillo* is the word we want. It would, very correctly, be called the *cerviguillo*, but almost never is.

Mozo de espada   Sword boy.

Muleta   The small red cape, stiffened with a rod, which is used by the *matador* during the final passes which lead to the kill. Only the *matador* can use the *muleta*.

Novillero   Apprentice matador.

Parado   A bull that is tired, cautious, wounded and liable to attack with cunning.

Parar   To stand one's ground.

Pase de pecho   Chest-high pass.

Pase natural   Cape pass which moves the cloth across the *toro*'s leading eye in a noseward direction.

Paseíllo   Prologue of the *corrida*, a parade involving all its human participants.

Peones   Assist the *matador* and must draw the bulls away from fallen or terror-struck men. Also known as a *banderillero*.

Peto   Heavy padding that protects the flanks and bellies of the *picadors*' horses.

Picador   Mounted *torero* armed with a lance—the *vara*. Allowed to wear gold braid on his jacket. Charged with piercing the bull during the *Suerte de Varas*.

Puyazo   Encounter between a bull and a *picador*'s lance.

Querencia   A favourite spot the bull will always return to.

Quite   The drawing-away of the bull by a *torero*.

Rebolera   Spectacular, spinning cape pass to finish a series. See *remate*.

Rejoneador   A *torero* who plays and spears the bull from horseback.

Rejoneo   Bull spectacle in which *rejoneadors* use lances to kill the bulls.

Remate   A finishing, flicking pass to fix the bull in place at the end of a series of cape passes.

Rubio   Ideal point for the *matador* to place his final, killing sword blow.

Rueda de peones   The swaying of *peones*' capes in an effort to make the bull move its head from side to side in order that the sword works through an artery.

Sentido   The bull's awareness that man is his enemy rather than the cloth of the cape.

Sorteo   Process whereby the six principal bulls in a *corrida* are assigned to *matadors* to produce an equality of form and performance in the ring.

Suerte   Variously defined as (good) luck, fortune, chance, destiny, lot.

Suerte de Banderillas   The second act of the *corrida*, in which *banderillas* are driven into the bull's back by the *banderilleros*.

Suerte de Matar   The final act of the *corrida*—the Act of the Kill. It is more usually known as the *faena*.

Suerte de Varas   The first act of the *corrida*—the Act of Spears.

Talleguilla   The embroidered britches of the *traje de luces*.

Tanda   A group of passes.

Templar   To govern the pace of the bull's actions, maintaining a fixed distance between the cloth and the bull's horns.

Temporada   The season for *corridas*.

Tendido   The "slopes" of seats in the plaza.

Tercio   An act of the corrida. (Also known as a *suerte*.)

Tienta   The test of immature *toros' casta* and *trapío* carried out on the *ganadería*.

Toreo   The art of playing the bulls in the *corrida*.

Torero   Sometimes used interchangeably with *matador*; it properly applies to any of the three classes of human participants in the *corrida*—the *matador* who kills the bull, the *picador* who is mounted and tests the bull with spear-thrusts, and the *peones* who assist the *matador*. A female *torero* would be a *tor-*

era, although this term isn't always popular with female *toreros*. In a very macho world it can seem to imply a certain inferiority.

Toril The holding pen where the bull is kept prior to its appearance in the ring. The *toril* gate is also known as the "Gate of Fear."

Toro bravo Literally, "brave bull"—the breed developed exclusively for use in the *corrida*. Also known as *toro de lidia*—"bull of struggle central to the corrida."

Toro de lidia See *toro bravo*.

Traje de luces "Suit of lights": the traditional garb of the *torero* in the ring.

Trapío A bull's physical conformation.

Vaquero Spanish cowboy.

Vara *Picador*'s long wooden pole, tipped with a spike, or *puya*.

Veronica A pass that involves holding the cape up in front of the body with both hands.

Zapatillas Flat black slippers.

Bibliography

For the information of opponents and friends of the corrida:

Killer of Bulls—The Autobiography of a Matador by Juan Belmonte, trans. Leslie Charteris
The Dangerous Summer by Ernest Hemingway
Death in the Afternoon by Ernest Hemingway
Death of a Matador by Barnaby Conrad
Bullfighting by John Fulton
The Complete Aficionado by John McCormick and Mario Sevilla Mascareñas
Taurina by Juan Miguel Sánchez Vigil and Manuel Durán Blázquez

The Internet also has an increasing variety of English-, French- and Spanish-language sites dealing with every aspect of the corrida. Many taurine magazines, including the well-known Spanish titles *Aplausos* and *Toros 6*, are available online.